D1466717

The Digital Revolution *in* Higher Education

How and Why the Internet of Everything is Changing Everything

Alan R. Shark

Executive Editor and Contributing Author

Written by leading professionals working the front lines of higher education

Published by Public Technology Institute • Alexandria, Virginia

Library of Congress Cataloging – Publication – Data

Shark, Alan R.
The Digital Revolution in Higher Education—
How and Why the Internet of Everything is Changing Everything

ISBN-13: 978-1511523714
ISBN-10: 1511523719

1. Distance education. 2. Education, Higher. 3. Internet in higher education. I. Title

Public Technology Institute
1420 Prince Street, Suite 200
Alexandria, Virginia 22314
www.pti.org

Contents

Preface

For years, thought leaders in higher education have warned of disruptive change looming on the horizon. And with the advent of massive open online courses, or MOOCs, many proclaimed that the forces of change had come to a head. Now that students could access high-quality courses on any topic, any time, anywhere—for free—what need would they have for a traditional college education?

Doomsdayers were convinced that professors would be replaced by video lectures. Venerable universities would crumble and shut down. Degrees would become valueless trinkets.

In reality, though, MOOCs have been less of a death sentence and more of a tool for a long-overdue revamp of the practice of teaching and learning in higher education. Innovative faculty have experimented with using MOOC content as a digital textbook, flipping the classroom by asking students to review recorded lectures in advance and reserving class time for more collaborative work. Some have run MOOCs and on-campus courses concurrently, allowing students to interact online with a global community of learners. Others have used the experience of teaching a MOOC to improve their brick-and-mortar courses, armed with new skills, technologies and techniques for engaging students. In many cases, these efforts have had a measurable, positive effect on student learning outcomes.

MOOCs are just one example of technology's impact on higher education. Students today have access to a dizzying array of tools for learning—and those tools are changing all the time. Take mobile technologies, for example: About 10 years ago, Duke University redefined mobile learning by handing out iPods to its entire freshman class. A few years later, Abilene Christian University did the same with iPhones, and then with iPads. How long until every college student is wearing an Apple watch?

It's important to mention, too, that these gadgets are not merely toys for attracting students' tuition dollars—they are part of comprehensive mobile initiatives focused on enhancing teaching and learning. Curricula are redesigned to leverage mobility; mobile apps enable collaboration and learning on the go; e-textbooks provide affordable, interactive learning materials; faculty receive support and resources to change the way they teach; and results are carefully monitored to evaluate what works best.

The fact is, colleges and universities that invest in mobile learning are responding to a fundamental truth: Technology has become ubiquitous in students' everyday lives, and institutions must adapt to students' technology expectations in order to stay relevant.

According to Refuel Agency, a research firm specializing in youth and niche consumer markets, the average college student owns seven technology devices (laptops and smartphones top the list of most popular items).[1] With the growing popularity of wearable tech, that figure could easily

---

[1] 2014 College Explorer survey; www.refuelagency.com/college-explorer

double in the next few years. The proliferation of devices is an opportunity not to be missed—a chance to innovate and embrace change.

Suppose a Google Glass-like product becomes the next must-have device—every college student comes to campus wearing a powerful computerized eyepiece. Students record video streams of their learning experiences, documenting their work in an immersive, authentic manner. (First-person video capture, by the way, is already happening in real-life Glass pilots at a few pioneering institutions.) Each learning moment is augmented with a visible backchannel of social media chatter or helpful information from the Web. With a flick of the wrist, a student can move learning content from his eyepiece to a larger classroom display for collaboration with peers, whether he is physically present or beaming in from afar. Faculty can tap into a rich stream of data from the devices, measuring subtle head movements, temperature changes, sleep patterns, breakfast habits and more to help determine students' comprehension of course material. Everything feeds into a limitless data repository, continuously updated and analyzed to support student success.

Is all that technology really necessary for learning? Of course not; students have passively listened to lectures for hundreds of years. But when a tool can make learning more interactive and engaging, increase access to more students, and identify and support students at risk of falling behind, it would be a shame not to use it.

— **Rhea Kelly, Executive Editor,**
Campus Technology **magazine**

Acknowledgments

Over a breakfast meeting in 2013, I had the pleasure of meeting Renee Patton, head of Cisco's US Public Sector Education efforts. We discussed the rapidly changing technology landscape that touches every aspect of education today. Thus a seed of greater collaboration and innovation was planted that ultimately led to the publishing of this book.

The purpose of the book is to examine the many beneficial aspects of the digital revolution currently underway. I am most grateful to Renee and her team, who have been wonderfully supportive and helpful. This highly motivated group includes Carol Stillman, Mary Schlegelmilch, Lance Ford, Celena Aponte, and Victoria Ryan. This book has been a wonderful collaboration effort between the Public Technology Institute and Cisco.

Of course I am most grateful to the 12 authors who took the time to write and share their experiences. Without their insights and first-hand experiences this book would not be possible.

I am also grateful to PTI's expert production team, which includes our copy editor Kathy O'Toole, seasoned editor, journalist, and former editor of the Stanford Business magazine. Sally Hoffmaster, PTI's senior go-to design professional, has received many awards for design and art and created the cover designs and the layout of every page for both print and e-reader versions of this book.

About PTI

Located in the greater Washington DC area, PTI was founded in 1971 and continues to actively support technology leadership for the public sector—in particular state and local government and more recently, higher education. The mission is carried out through thought-leadership publications, research, education services, executive level consulting services, training and certification programs, as well as awards and recognition programs. PTI also offers online educational programs throughout the year and maintains a dynamic relationship with Rutgers University-Newark's School of Public Affairs and Administration. For more information, see www.pti.org.

Introduction

Towards the University of Everything?

Higher education has come under increasing scrutiny as never before due to rising costs, changes in future job requirements, and new forms of learning opportunities offered by non-traditional companies and institutions. Students and parents are rightfully questioning the value of higher education based on perceived outcomes as well as staggering student loans that in some cases could take a lifetime to pay back. While the value equation debate rages on, there is another phenomenon taking place. It is nothing short of a revolution regarding the advances in technology and how institutions of higher learning along with nontraditional organizations are utilizing these powerful new tools. These new tools include new mobile devices, enhanced and feature-rich learning management systems, data-feeding sensors, 3D printers, smart classrooms, smart buildings, and collaboration tools allowing students and faculty to collaborate just about anywhere face-to-face, virtually.

Today a faculty member could develop an entire online course through iTunes University or Blackboard that is easy to use and template-driven. Kahn University as well as other specialized learning companies that offer free programs rely on YouTube, which has over three billion users with over 300 hours of video being uploaded each and every minute. Thousands of educational institutions and programs regularly store lectures, courses, and interviews online for all to see.

The Digital Revolution in Higher Education—How and Why the Internet of Everything is Changing Everything is designed to be thought-provoking as it examines the many dimensions and perspectives of the innovator, the student, the faculty, the administrator, and more as we explore this exciting topic. We begin our journey with Brett Trusko, faculty member at three universities and CEO of the International Association of Innovation Professionals, who sets the stage. Then lest we get too carried away, Stuart Butler, of the Brookings Institution, provides a sobering and critical view of the economic outlook for higher education and the ensuing options. When his piece first appeared in the American Interest in 2014, I contacted Dr. Butler right away seeking permission to reprint—it remains a timely and provocative addition.

The faculty perspective, written with input from other faculty members, points out how technology is impacting the classroom and in particular, the iconic one dimensional lecture. Both Lance Ford and Mary Schlegelmilch describe some of the key issues that may be preventing faster adoption of new technologies aimed at enriching the teaching and learning experience. They also point out what still needs to happen and why.

Having a view from the CIO of a leading university helps add to the narrative as Tracy Futhey shares her experiences and challenges as head of information technology at Duke University. The view of a college university president Mohammad Qayoumi, at San Jose University reminds us how challenging it is to foster change—especially when it comes to the realities of adopting greater technology solutions. Dr. Qayoumi laments about the university governance structure that almost assures moving slowly—no matter how a president tries to make changes. And then there are the students. Celena Aponte is an instructor and very close to students, enabling her to precisely capture some of key student likes and dislikes.

The Digital revolution in higher education is moving far beyond the traditional campus as nonprofits, and corporations are seeking ways to satisfy unmet needs. Ronda Mosley points out that part of this interest is aimed at trying to plug immediate gaps in skill sets for jobs that need to be filled. Another aspect of corporate involvement and interest is the need for learning new skills through specialized courses or certifications. Corporations like Cisco, Intel, GE, Ford, and others have focused on *STEM* or *STEAM* learning programs as part of their corporate responsibility programs. We are already witnessing a number of higher education-focused public private partnerships aimed at improving learning outcomes as well as making increasing the reach of postsecondary education to unserved segments of the US population.

While recruiting and compiling this book, I was introduced to Ray Smith and Steve Wunderli who remind us that learning is more than just about technology and devices, and that to truly learn and absorb, one must also have a social component. One of the best methods may be through the time-tested technique called storytelling. Add technology to enhance storytelling and you have a winning strategy. Today we find ourselves saturated with content from music, entertainment, games, shared pictures, Ted Talks, podcasts, cable, and of course YouTube. The bottom line is the best way to learn and absorb is through good storytelling.

Finally Renee Patton and Carol Stillman provide a very useful framework for assessing what one might have today and to begin planning for tomorrow. None of us who have worked on this book project view this edition as a comprehensive view of where we are today and where we should be headed tomorrow, but we all agree this effort is a starting point. Rather than pile on to much of the negative commentary where the line grows longer, we like to think of this work as adding to a more positive dialog. Simply put, when technology is used wisely it can save money in the long run and greatly improve the learning experience—from almost anywhere, to almost anyone.

Chapter 1

The Future and Present Challenges of Higher Education

Chapter 1
The Future and Present Challenges of Higher Education

By Brett E. Trusko

Higher education is on the verge of profound change. The bastion of new ideas is failing to keep up with the demands of a changing world—a world of innovation and technology. Funding for education is decreasing, while the average time it takes for a student to graduate is going up for all degree programs. The perceived need for a college education is diminishing with many of the most notable and successful entrepreneurs of our time; they are either bypassing college completely or dropping out without completing their bachelor's degrees.

Imagine a new educational system where someone could and would float in and out of campus, attending some classes in a live format and some virtually. Perhaps they would have the opportunity to virtually attend the class of a world-renowned political scientist from home, then run down to the campus of their university for a calculus class, then drive across town to another university for an engineering class, and finish the day in a local tavern for a free, fully automated instructor-less computer programming class. Best yet, all these venues could be consolidated into a single degree program from a highly respected university that acted more like a project management office than a traditional university—one that enabled students to get what they needed, when they needed it, and where they needed it.

This future is playing out in many small ways throughout the world today. Going to college used to mean that you left home, moved many miles away, lived in a dorm, and finished a degree in four years. In the autumn of your senior year, employers would come to the campus and set up tables and book rooms where interviews could be held; and if you were fortunate enough, the company you really wanted to work for would invite you to its offices for interviews. If you were hired, the company would keep your training up to date, and you would have a job for the rest of your life.

Starting around the end of the 1980s, all this began to change. Companies started to lay people off when business slowed down, and layoffs caught on throughout the business world. Too many jobs over the course of a career looked bad on a resume 30 years ago, but that has changed so that now you may be turned down for a job if you do not have enough jobs on your resume. Employees began to own their own computers and mobile phones (BYOE—bring your own equipment). The knowledge worker, in many cases, has become like the craftsman who utilizes the equipment they prefer to use instead of the equipment they are forced to use by their employers. While stealing corporate secrets is still frowned upon, much of what people create stays with them as they move along their career path. In fact, with the advent of portable data-storage drives, it no longer makes sense for employers to expect that some of what employees produce is not staying with them.

So, this sets the stage for the topic of this chapter and book. With employed individuals becoming more like free agents than traditional employees, students and then employees are more interested in what a gig can do for them instead of lifetime employment. This flows in both directions, begging the questions of efficiency and effectiveness in the educational options one considers.

Most universities still offer something they like to refer to as the core curriculum. For example, at Texas A&M, every student must complete the following on their way to a bachelor's degree (in anything):

- Communications (6 hours)
- Mathematics (6 hours)
- Natural sciences (8 hours)
- Humanities (3 hours)
- Visual and performing arts (3 hours)
- Social and behavioral sciences (3 hours)
- U.S. history and political science (6 hours of each)
- International and cultural diversity (6 hours)

These core classes represent 51 credit hours (out of approximately 120) outside of your required major. Therefore, if you are a computer science major, you are required to take roughly half of your classes outside what you choose to do with your life and career. We personally feel that these classes serve to graduate more well-rounded students; but in a competitive world where college is increasingly expensive and employers are less and less satisfied with the results of a four-year education, can this really continue? As we interviewed people about the topic, we found out that Cisco Systems must train network engineers for a year before putting them in a productive position. National Oilfield Varco must train their petroleum engineers for two years above and beyond the four-year degree that the student has just earned. To make this even worse, highly successful modern companies like Google are indicating that they aren't really big on college degrees any longer, stating that they "value skills and experiences" more than degrees.[1] They don't completely write off college since these are places to gain skills and experiences, but they specifically state that they consider the following when assessing a candidate:

- **General cognitive ability**
  (not I.Q., but the ability to learn)
- **Leadership**
  (emergent leadership versus traditional leadership)
- **Humility**
  (admitting that you don't know everything)
- **Ownership**
  (fight for what you believe in and take a stand)
- **Expertise**
  (but this is the least important).

Now let's take a look at each of these and see how they fit into a traditional college education.

General cognitive ability—it has now been demonstrated time and time again that a college education is not a requirement for success. Take our most famous examples of college dropouts (or those who never went—and they are not all technology people):

---

[1] Thomas Friedman. "How to Get a Job at Google," *New York Times,* February 22, 2014. http://www.nytimes.com/2014/02/23/opinion/sunday/friedman-how-to-get-a-job-at-google.html

- **Sheldon Adelson,** *billionaire casino owner*
- **Paul Allen,** *cofounder of Microsoft*
- **Micky Arison,** *chairman of Carnival Cruise Lines*
- **Jane Austen,** *novelist*
- **Steve Ballmer,** *Microsoft CEO, owner of the Seattle Seahawks*
- **Ronald Baron,** *founder of Baron Capital*
- **Eike Batista,** *billionaire mining executive*
- **Anne Beiler,** *founder of Auntie Anne's Pretzels*
- **Carl Bernstein,** *reporter*
- **Patrrizio Bertelli,** *cofounder of Prada*
- **Zak Boca,** *cofounder of SingleHop*
- **Richard Branson,** *founder of Virgin Music, Mobile, Airways, etc.*
- **Sergey Brin,** *cofounder of Google*
- **Warren Buffet,** *chairman of Berkshire Hathaway*
- **Robert Byrd,** *U.S. senator*
- **James Francis Byrnes,** *U.S. representative, senator, Supreme Court justice, secretary of state, and South Carolina governor*

And these are just the people whose names start with a B. Other highly notable individuals lacking college credentials include: Winston Churchill, Grover Cleveland, Michael Dell, Walt Disney, Thomas Edison, Albert Einstein, Larry Ellison, William Faulkner, John F. Kennedy (eight U.S. Presidents had no college degree), Henry Ford, Bill Gates, Barry Goldwater, Peter Jennings, Steve Jobs, John Mackey, George Orwell, Joel Osteen, Larry Page, John D. Rockefeller Sr., Karl Rove, George Bernard Shaw, Ted Turner, Steve Wozniak, Jerry Yang, and, of course, Mark Zuckerberg.

They are all drop-outs who could probably land a job in Silicon Valley, but probably not at IBM. Demonstrated cognitive ability? Absolutely! Leadership? Without a doubt! As for humility, ownership, and expertise—well those are hard to assess, but based on the general lack of formal education, you would guess that at some point, the majority of them experienced humility; and ownership and expertise may not have been a part of them in the beginning, but they all certainly possessed it at some time.

The point is that the societal mores are shifting so that results mean more than education, and sometimes education is waste of time for people who have an idea or motivation that can't be put on a shelf for four years or more.

So, how have we gotten to where we are today? This chapter discusses the opportunities facing students and educators as we continue forward in the 21st century—issues such as efficiency in education, the shifting norms of society toward technology skills, and the need to consume education in new and effective ways.

Budgetary Limitations

America's higher education system is becoming less affordable for the middle class, due in large part to the loss of public funding. In fact, between 2006 and 2007 alone, the rate of investment in public higher education dropped by 12.5%. Sharp tuition increases have become the norm, with tuition for California public institutions increasing by 98% between

2006 and 2010.[2] As education becomes more expensive, the out-of-pocket cost to parents and increasing student loans that mortgage students' futures have pushed many to look for a better educational deal.

The one-two financial punch attached to higher education is a slow and steady increase in the cost of overhead at universities. A November 21, 2012 article in *Business Week* notes that during the period between 1992 and 2009, the average increase in administrators at U.S. schools has increased 60%, while the number of faculty has only increased 6%. Using Purdue University as an example at the time the article was written, administrator salaries (not including the president or provost), ranged from $253,000 to $433,000, while the average salary for a full professor was less than $125,000.[3] This raises the question of whether education is improving in the United States or not. While *U.S. News and World Report* ranks U.S. institutions of higher education as some of the best in the world, there are many indications that they are slipping, or at least that the rest of the world is catching up.

A 2013 article in *The Atlantic,* contains a table that is a snapshot of performance in mathematics, reading and science (see next page).

As one can see from the table, the U.S. is ranked only as average in international standardized tests. Contrary to the *U.S.*

---

[2] Dylan Fisher. "Funding Higher Ed: Three Solutions," *University Business,* Feb 2013, http://www.universitybusiness.com/article/funding-higher-ed-three-solutions

[3] Hechinger, John "The Troubling Dean-to-Professor Ratio." *Bloomberg Business,* Nov 21, 2012, http://www.bloomberg.com/bw/articles/2012-11-21/the-troubling-dean-to-professor-ratio

Snapshot of performance in mathematics, reading and science

☐ Countries/economies with a mean performance/share of top performers above the OECD average, countries/economies with a share of low achievers below the OECD average

☐ Countries/economies with a mean performance/share of low achievers/share of top performers not statistically significantly different from the OECD average

☐ Countries/economies with a mean performance/share of top performers below the OECD average, countries/economies with a share of low achievers above the OECD average

	MATHEMATICS				READING		SCIENCE	
	Mean score in PISA 2012	Share of low achievers in mathematics (Below Level 2)	Share of top performers in mathematics (Level 5 or 6)	Annualised change in score points	Mean score in PISA 2012	Annualised change in score points	Mean score in PISA 2012	Annualised change in score points
OECD average	494	23.1	12.6	-0.3	496	0.3	501	0.5
Shanghai-China	613	3.8	55.4	4.2	570	4.6	580	1.8
Hong-Kong China	561	8.5	33.7	1.3	545	2.3	555	2.1
Korea	554	9.1	30.9	1.1	536	0.9	538	2.6
Japan	536	11.1	23.7	0.4	538	1.5	547	2.6
Switzerland	531	12.4	21.4	0.6	509	1.0	515	0.6
Canada	518	13.8	16.4	-1.4	523	-0.9	525	-1.5
Poland	518	14.4	16.7	2.6	518	2.8	526	4.6
Germany	514	17.7	17.5	1.4	508	1.8	524	1.4
Denmark	500	16.8	10.0	-1.8	496	0.1	498	0.4
France	495	22.4	12.9	-1.5	505	0.0	499	0.6
United Kingdom	494	21.8	11.8	-0.3	499	0.7	514	-0.1
Portugal	487	24.9	10.6	2.8	488	1.6	489	2.5
Russian Federation	482	24.0	7.8	1.1	475	1.1	486	1.0
United States	481	25.8	8.8	0.3	498	-0.3	497	1.4
Israel	466	33.5	9.4	4.2	486	3.7	470	2.8
United Arab Emirates	434	46.3	3.5	m	442	m	448	m
Thailand	427	49.7	2.6	1.0	441	1.1	444	3.9
Mexico	413	54.7	0.6	3.1	424	1.1	415	0.9
Argentina	388	66.5	0.3	1.2	396	-1.6	415	2.4
Qatar	376	69.6	2.0	9.2	388	12.0	384	5.4

The annualized change is the average annual change in PISA score points from a country's/economy's earliest participation in PISA to PISA 2012. It is calculated taking into account all of a country's/economy's participation in PISA.

NOTE: Countries/economies in which the annualised change in performance is statistically significant are marked in bold. Countries and economies are ranked in descending order of the mean mathematics score in PISA 2012.

SOURCE: OECD, PISA 2012 Database

News and World Report article, the best colleges in the world may be located in the United States, but the average university in the United States does no better than the average school worldwide. Essentially, it may be said that the growing divide between the haves and the have-nots that is being discussed over and over in the news seems to apply to our system of higher ed. Those that get into the best schools in the U.S. are probably receiving the best education in the world, while the average student is likely to be receiving something less than average.

Finally, higher education is failing to recruit the best and the brightest faculty. As shown in the *Business Week* article, the salaries of professors have not kept up with administrators' salaries; and less known to many, the perks that once made lower salaries palatable, such as reduced or free tuition for family members, and reasonable expectations for tenure, have all but disappeared. Successful academics today are rewarded for research and federal grants, and not for teaching. And this is happening in a time when grant funding is decreasing, leading to established researchers winning a larger share of grant money and elbowing out early career researchers—in effect dooming the system to educators who will accept less money and stability. Of course, this would portend even worse performance for higher education in the future.

Technology

This chapter, although starting with a down tone, is not a story of failure, but is a story of hope about higher education and its potential to be exactly what students and employers hope it will be. As is the case with so much change these days, it is technology that will allow the system to reform and deliver what the world needs.

Let's take the case of Uber as an example of what technology can do for higher ed. While many may think Uber is a story of disruption (and it is to a certain extent), it is also an important story of what can be done with idle resources. Take the case of New York City. Anyone who has spent a significant amount of time there knows that at certain times of day it is impossible to find a cab. While this is a simple case of supply and demand, because cabbies usually work 12-hour shifts, there are periods when there are too many cabs and periods when there are too few. If you put enough cabs on the road to handle peak demand, there are a considerable number of cabs driving around during non-peak hours without passengers, wasting time and money and polluting the environment. Uber simply uses a large number of personal cars and effectively deploys them during peak hours. One could still take a cab during those peak hours and pay a lower fare than for an Uber car, but as anyone who has had to get to the airport during rush hour in New York can tell you, an expensive ride is always better than no ride. It is the consumer's choice.

Uber is a pure technology play that recognizes, among other things, that there are excess resources that are not deployed. How is this any different than the campus in almost any university in America during holiday breaks or summer vacation? What about the limited seats available at the most selective universities in the country?

Technology deals with this and so many other infrastructure differences in ways that are only bounded by the imagination. At the core of this change is the internet, which allows a connectedness that has never been experienced in the history of the world. Take, for example, the International Association of Innovation Professionals (IAOIP) which we started in 2013, and which, in less than a year, had members in more than 21 countries. The association is, in many ways, the kind of organization that will challenge the modern higher education model. Enabled by the internet, members can join the association, use the material generated by its working groups, and be certified as an innovation professional. If you compare this to a college certification, you have roughly the same process. A student applies/member joins, they take classes/utilize the material of the association, and then take exams, which lead to a certificate that claims the student/member is qualified to apply what he or she has learned. In many ways, this isn't unlike the trades in the last century. After all, it wasn't long ago that physicians didn't even go to medical school and instead just apprenticed as a medical doctor.

So, the velocity that the internet creates allows business models to change in profound ways—Amazon's model for books; iTunes, for music; and so on. Why can't this change also take place in education?

Another distinct advantage enabled by technology is almost-infinite scalability. Once again, using the IAOIP as an example, a traditional university creates a land-locked venture that forces students to leave home, move to the university, and attend classes in buildings, usually named after successful alumni. A college president once told me that he she didn't need more donations for buildings. What she really needed were donations to pay for the janitors, heating, cooling, and repairs on the buildings that were already donated. The fixed cost associated with higher education may be one of the biggest problems they actually face in the future, and the model is not even remotely scalable. A university built to hold 50,000 students may be minimally scalable; accordingly, there will always be forces attempting to limit the scalability.

Scalability, if it is a possibility in a university, can take several paths. One is the extension of the online course catalogue. This means that there are more classes taught by a professor to remote students. Traditionally, this has only been an extension of the current model applied to a virtual classroom. The drawback to this is that most professors do not like the format and demand that the virtual classroom be the same size as the traditional classroom. If their current live version of the class accommodates 30 students, then the online course also holds 30 students. (In reality, most professors prefer their online classes be smaller due to the issues of managing 24/7 communications.) To reach scalability, universities must utilize technology with platforms such as massive open online courses, known as MOOCs. (This is not to be confused with Mook, which means a stupid or incompetent person, although it begs the question of whether the inventor of the MOOC acronym had a double meaning.) We digress though. Under the current model of testing and proof of competency, having a thousand students all take an exam with a free-text answer becomes impossible for a single instructor. This is even a limitation at the IAOIP. Imagine the problems a professor would encounter if his or her MOOC had 1,000 students from all over the world and had only a single essay question of 500 words. This equates to 500,000 words that must be read by an individual or analyzed by a computer. As a frame of reference, last year Yale economist Robert Shiller taught a MOOC with more than 120,000 students in a single class. At 500 words per student, Shiller would have to process 60 million words, which is the equivalent of more than 100 copies of *War and Peace.*

Therefore, while MOOCs may be touted as the answer to education scalability, and even if there were no problems associated with exams that contained only multiple-choice questions, the sheer volume of students becomes a problem if the instructor wants to reach the students in conventional ways.

Many universities are now comfortable with telepresence as a strategy for teaching. This allows students to remain in separate geographical locations, but still allows the instructor to be communicating directly. Once again however, the scalability is extremely limited.

So, in the end we are faced with the same types of problems we have had all along with venue and being land locked, literally and virtually, by faculty reach and the ability to communicate, examine, and certify (through a grade) that the student has mastered the subject.

In our research for this chapter, we have seen a few interesting things, such as the library at Lone Star College in Houston, Texas, which no longer has any books. A relaxed environment with sofas and comfortable chairs, this library feels more like a clean Starbucks coffee shop. In fact, if you were to look at the traditional library, you will find stacks and stacks of books that no one is using. Most students simply go online, so why even have the books in the stacks? While we are sure that there are many university libraries that have done away with books, this is the first we have seen, and the entire library seems much more functional for the way people actually study.

Another interesting phenomenon at Lone Star College, a two-year community college, is a co-location program with two local universities that offer four-year degrees. Previously, we had seen high school kids traveling periodically to a university to take classes, and we had even seen community colleges offering classes that earn credit at a four-year college, but we had never seen a university co-located within a community college so that a student can seamlessly move from a two-year to a four-year school without leaving campus.

These observations from Lone Star College are just a few examples of how to utilize technology to scale the educational experience. Once the library gets rid of books, what is to stop the university from closing it all together, and perhaps just adding seats to the coffee shop or cafeteria?

Essentially, we are land locked in a university that is established to service a model that requires students to come to a location, whether in real life or virtually, and take a class that is not at all tailored to the needs of the student.

Change in Student and Societal Attitudes

The whole question of the future of higher education becomes really interesting when we begin to examine the changing expectations of students and society as a whole. In a world that seems to be losing faith in the professions (and we will call professorship a profession), where does one go to receive what they need, when they need it, and how they need it? As an example, the long-running television series *Two and a Half Men,* features a character who is a multi-billionaire who dropped out of college. The stories of Steve Jobs, Bill Gates, and the Google founders make it seem almost cool never to finish college. We can refer to this age as the age of the *internet entrepreneur,* and some of those entrepreneurs found success without a college degree. While the vast majority of successful individuals these days do have college degrees, there are many people who are just in too much of a hurry to finish college. After all, there are always plenty of MBAs you can hire if you need them.

This raises the question of whether investment in a college education is still as valuable as it used to be. Consider the implications of the term "internet time," which is commonly used to refer to something condensed or accelerated. We've always had people in the entertainment world who skipped college because the opportunities to make money in that business do not necessarily require a formal education. When a young person is a skilled programmer and can develop an application without the benefit of formal programming classes, what does the education add? In the case of the aforementioned internet entrepreneurs, the investment world happily funds someone with a good idea because business people can always be hired. The same principle is true in areas such as art and music. Yes, going to expensive art school or music school may teach you to be a better musician or artist; but tell that to the many rock stars who are multimillionaires. Anyone who suggested the artist would have been more successful more quickly with formal training has little empirical evidence to support the claim.

So why has college become the cornerstone of our society? There are many theories, but perhaps the single theme that would radiate through all of them is that college is the equivalent of "punching your ticket." For example, consider an accountant. There are many established accounting rules and procedures. One could argue that having a standardized education in generally accepted accounting principles is critical to the functioning of our financial system. Granted, an accountant could learn on the job; however, being awarded an accounting degree from an accredited school and then passing the CPA exam seems like a much better strategy than learning on the job. This is not to say there are no excellent accountants without a college degree. It's just that it makes more sense for someone like an accountant to be trained in a standard manner by professionals. This also seems to be a good strategy for positions such as doctors, lawyers, and engineers. Of course Leonardo da Vinci never attended school and appears to have done quite well as an engineer. But he did not have to function in the modern world where professional certifications were mandatory, and the ramifications of failed engineering have such dire consequences.. One could argue that perhaps Leonardo would've been a better engineer if he had learned engineering principles. But this can also be a circular reference; others might argue he was so good precisely because he never received a formal education. While we recognize the master's degree in business administration as a valuable educational credential, one would probably find very few of them in the ranks of successful entrepreneurs.

Here is where the question of degrees from universities becomes so important. If our world is changing in a way that values results in an efficient an effective manner, the current iteration of higher education is very likely wrong. Let's take this a step further.

As we discussed earlier, companies such as Cisco Systems and National Oilfield Varco (NOV) require one year and two-years (respectively) of additional training for their net-work engineers and petroleum engineers before they feel like they can put them into productive service. In the case of a network engineer, this means the company needs to invest approximately $150,000 above and beyond what they've already paid in taxes to support public education. Imagine for a moment, the companies decided that they shouldn't have to pay for the additional training for these people. Imagine that Cisco called this first year an apprenticeship. As an apprentice, the new hire would receive little or no pay for that first year. How would students feel about their college education if employers specifically said it wasn't adequate? As we travel around and talk to companies about this question it appears that this is actually the case: Additional training has become a part of doing business. What companies are telling us is that they're looking for employees with skills and not necessarily degrees.

Let's consider the certification of skills such as those required of a project manager. The generally agreed-upon expert organization for project managers is the Project Management Institute, or PMI for short. There are also dozens of universities that offer a degree in project management. If I am an employer and would like an employee to gain the skills of project management, would I be better off sending that employee back to college for four years at a cost of $100,000, or sending them to training so they can become PMI certified in six weeks for $20,000? To make matters worse for conventional colleges, even if the employee has a degree in project management, it is likely that he or she will still have to pass the PMI examination to be taken seriously as a project manager. This example is a bit soft because the reality is that there are skilled project managers who have no project management training from a university, nor have they taken training from the Project Management Institute. On a more serious side, to participate in the audit of a publicly traded company one must possess a certified public accountant certification (CPA). To sit for the CPA examination requires a four-year college degree. In the case of the CPA, it makes sense if you receive a college education in accounting; but in the case of the PMI, a degree is not a prerequisite.

Engineering firms must consider liability issues when they hire engineers to design bridges, buildings, and other products. While there may be people who are fully capable of designing a bridge without having an engineering degree, imagine the risk the company takes if it employs engineers who were not college trained and have not completed professional engineering certification. If the bridge fails, even for reasons that have nothing to do with the engineering, the risk of losing a lawsuit is great for the engineering firm.

But think about this in the context of some of the newer jobs that have surfaced in the last few years. Have you ever read the disclaimer on software? What about when you update the software on your smartphone? If you actually read the disclaimer (which few people do, by the way), you will find out that the company takes almost no responsibility for what might go wrong if the program fails. Nowhere is this risk greater than in the electronic healthcare record industry. Vendors of electronic healthcare software make the same claims that app developers for your smartphone do. Generally speaking, their argument is that every healthcare provider is different, so the record vendors can't possibly create a program that would completely eliminate the possibility of medical error by the program. Instead, they state that medical professionals should be responsible for assuring the correct drugs, dosages, and treatments, are listed in a record. After all, the programmers don't know medicine.

Even newer certifications do not accept liability for the certified person. For example, the Project Management Institute does not accept any liability for people who are certified as a project manager.. In the case of PMI and IAOIP, certification merely affirms that the person knows the body of knowledge and generally how to apply it. PMI does not warrant the certified project manager is, in fact, a good project manager nor does the IAOIP warrant that the innovation professional is an innovator. All that's warranted is that the person knows the body of knowledge and how to apply it in given situations. Once again, this basic question arises: How is this any different than a college education? Does the university assume responsibility for an engineer, trained at their university, when a bridge designed by one of their graduates falls down? What universities do warrant is that the class required by the accrediting organization was taught by professors who have demonstrated mastery and the student passed all the tests. Is there any real difference between the student who is taught by a professor and one who is self-trained and learned from the same book? We would argue that it really makes no difference to employers.

Granted, there are employers that will only hire graduates from certain universities, but these are becoming fewer and farther between. A fictional example of this is the Lifetime network show *Suits,* which takes place in a fictional New York law firm that only hires graduates of Harvard. In the show, one of the best attorneys in the office has a secret. That secret is that he didn't go to Harvard. Funny thing in the show, however: I don't recall a client ever mentioning that they hired the firm because all of their students went to Harvard Law School. What's also ironic about the show is that the best attorney in the office never went to college at all. Instead, he's a very smart individual with very good knowledge of the law. As casual Fridays start to break down some of the workplace formality, and companies loosen wardrobe rules (IBM employees no longer are required to wear blue suits and white shirts), we may begin to see a true meritocracy in places other than Silicon Valley.

Currently, however, we maintain a cultural respect for college degrees. This may never change, and perhaps it shouldn't. The reality is that for every Steve Jobs at Apple there are tens of thousands of employees who did go to college. So I talk about the failure of college when the reality remains that most people *should* attend college. The most important point of this chapter isn't that college is failing; it's just the college is failing to be as effective and efficient as it should be. As stated, there are very important reasons for accountants, doctors, and engineers to go to college. And for every CFO in an organization there are dozens of college-trained accountants and bookkeepers supporting the organization. This extends to human resources, and the majority of administrative functions within most organizations. What we might really need from higher education in the future is to be redesigned to accommodate the world that moves faster and offers an education that is efficient as well as inexpensive. To remain competitive with the rest of the world, we all know that an education system has to be effective, but what few people realize is that it also needs to be efficient. When students in one country are able to achieve a benchmark in four years while it takes students in another country five years, this could be a problem of effectiveness or efficiency or both.

As an example, there used to be a joke amongst college students that they were on the "five-year plan." The fact is, today the average student takes approximately six years to graduate,[4] which is a very bad way for a young person to start adult life. There can be a number of reasons why graduation is delayed, including:

- Jobs and internships
- Overcrowded classrooms and poor schedules
- Easily accessible loans

With the increasing cost of college, more and more students are finding that they need to take jobs just to get by. While students have historically worked while in college, they tended to be part-time jobs in places like the bookstore. Today, students find it more difficult to work part-time jobs and place a higher value on internships, which many times are not even paid. Having to hold down full-time jobs while working obviously reduces the amount of classes a student can take.

It's not uncommon today for students to complain the classes that they need for graduation are closed. There are several contributing factors to this problem, including many of the ones mentioned above. For example, we are aware of a local business school that has 21 professor positions. In an average business school, salary for professors may be

[4] Luckerson, Victor. "The Myth of the Four-Year College Degree," *TimeMagazine*, Jan.10, 2013 http://business.time.com/2013/01/10/the-myth-of-the-4-year-college-degree/

$70,000 or less per year. When a professional receives a Ph.D. in business, even if they very much want to teach, there are plenty of other jobs in the market that pay more. This leads to a chronic shortage of certain types of professors in certain fields. Add to this the earlier discussion of administration ratios and the failure of salaries to keep up for professors, and in certain fields we do not have enough faculty to meet student demand.

The third problem is that of easily accessible loans. In our interviews, we discovered that many students stayed in school because they can continue to receive loans as long as they were students. This is particularly bothersome when a student has no declared major and, after four years, hasn't decided what he or she wants to do after graduating.

Not only is delayed graduation a problem for students, it is also a problem for taxpayers. When students take 50% more time to graduate than usual and take out student loans and grants to pay for that education, they cost taxpayers money. Additionally, delayed graduation adds costs that are difficult to quantify. For example, students who were in school for two years longer than necessary are not earning money or paying income taxes, and are potentially delaying their own retirement due to a lack of savings. From the government side, this is two years when a student should be working, earning a good living, and contributing to the tax base. While we couldn't find documentation related to the personal lives of the students who graduate late, we also believe that the longer it takes to graduate the less likely it is that it will happen. In many of our third tier universities throughout the United States, graduation rates are extremely low. In an interview, one university dean said that less than 25% of his institution's students graduated. Unfortunately, the United States has had to address a problem with for-profit universities that keep failing students in programs long enough to exhaust their student loan benefits. The default rate on student loans is a serious and potentially devastating reality in society today.

The Fun Stuff

Now that all the gloom and doom has been discussed, it's time for the fun stuff. While higher education may have its challenges, it could be an awesome time to be in the business. Students today may be more serious about their education than ever, and, take it from a couple of business executives, they are very smart! All over the world, the entrepreneurial spirit is taking root in ways never seen before. In all of our years, we've never seen so many extraordinary ideas presented to us on a daily basis. Many of these ideas are not that great, but many of them are outstanding. In the for-profit education space, there are a number of institutions that are doing an excellent job. The University of Phoenix has probably educated more MBAs than any other single school has. We have worked with these graduates, and while some are average, many are very smart professionals who saw the value in a University of Phoenix MBA over a bigger name school. The Khan Academy has very good programs for K-12 students in math, science, and other subjects. Sal Khan has brought together some of the best minds in a number of subjects and created interesting and interactive programs that educate in ways that are novel and interesting to students.

In industries all over the world, we see that integration is a significant opportunity. Take for example, the company Sprinklr, which offers software as a service (Saas). Specifically, Sprinklr bills itself as a social media management system (SMMS) that can consolidate the many social media inputs and outputs of major corporations. Considering only one social media platform, Twitter, they monitor all incoming posts and route them to the appropriate person or department who would be interested. On the outgoing side, they use advanced analytics to decide what messages should go out and what time of day to which audiences. This isn't the amazing part. What's amazing is they do this over approximately 30 social media platforms.

We were recently made aware of an organization that consolidates underground seismic maps from various oil company explorations. On their own, the companies would not consolidate the maps because they are competitors to each other. In fact, the time, expense, and capital investment of creating seismic maps is so high that sharing them with the competition doesn't make sense at the company level. However, at the consolidated level the oil companies are willing to give away the maps in return for the maps of their competitors. By bringing the maps from different companies together into a single map, the value of the individual maps are multiplied many times.

Everywhere you look consolidation is happening. Amazon is not only becoming the largest bookseller in the world, but the biggest distributor of their competitors' products. On the internet, scale is no longer a problem. In fact, economies of scale become hyper-realized.

One place where consolidation is noticeably lacking is in the education space. Each college and university is an island unto itself. A common complaint with four-year universities is in the difficulty of evaluating courses from other universities. In the university game, it really is winner take all. By this we mean that the university where you finally receive your degree is the sole consolidator of your education. If you attend more than two universities to receive a college degree, it is likely that you will lose a number of your course credits. In essence, you play by the rules of the university you graduate from. While this isn't an altogether bad idea, it isn't necessarily the way things are being done anymore.

Consider this: There are classes that lend themselves well to classroom settings. These classes might include calculus or engineering. There are other classes that could be offered online without the intervention of a professor. Such a class might be music appreciation. In the typical music appreciation class, students come to class, listen to music, and discuss the composer, artist, time period, etc. It's not a far stretch to imagine this class being delivered completely online. The student logs in when he or she feels in the mood to listen to music and spends an hour listening to the piece, followed by a recorded lecture by the professor. Since the typical music appreciation class might play the music and ask the student to identify the composer, the time period, and other details related to the music, the class lends itself very well to being done on the students' own time and at their own pace. Why a student would need to come to the university to attend this type of class could be debated. We in no way mean to diminish the importance of the music professor, only to point out that this type of class lends itself well to mass delivery.

Given the previous paragraph, let's go back and examine the core curriculum at Texas A&M University. If you recall from earlier in the chapter, the core curriculum look something like this:

- Communications (6 hours)
- Mathematics (6 hours)
- Natural sciences (8 hours)
- Humanities (3 hours)
- Visual and performing arts (3 hours)
- Social and behavioral sciences (3 hours)
- U.S. history and political science (6 hours of each)
- International and cultural diversity (6 hours)

Of this core curriculum, what might be good candidates for streamlining the student's classroom time? In communications, you might easily be able to take a writing class online, while a speech class may need to stay in a classroom. In math, perhaps being in the classroom full time is the best approach; but classroom time supplemented with excellent online tutorials in the subject may make the entire experience more enjoyable for students. In the natural sciences, classes could go either way, with the same requirement for outstanding tutorials. Obviously, lab time might be difficult to do outside the university, but just as we have seen a growth in *maker spaces* all over the world, perhaps we'll soon see *maker labs*—places where aspiring young chemists and biologists can go to work on their experiments. Depending on the humanities taken, the venue could vary. Depending on the subject and professor, who's to say that classes such as philosophy, history, literature, and languages couldn't be taken off campus? Visual and performing arts are another area that can vary by the course. Assuming music appreciation as part of the performing arts department, it could be online. A good percentage of the social and behavioral sciences could be offered online. Once again, the nature of the class will dictate whether or not it makes sense to move it out of the classroom. If a political science class is purely about the history of politics, it may be appropriate to take online. If the class is about creating a philosophical debate among students, it's highly likely that this class will be in the classroom. In the case of international and cultural diversity, some universities would be well served to offer these programs in a mixed community. Obviously, every class isn't the same, but the point is that there are classes that might be offered across many universities, time zones, and even countries.

The opportunity to make classes more portable is just the beginning. There are software packages available that allow admissions offices to more easily cross reference classes that can be considered equivalent. As a first start, this is an excellent way to begin standardizing courses across institutions. When this is set up under a software-as-a-service model, updates can be constantly fed into the system, and schools can continuously modify their own personal preferences. Under the current operating system, this is a very good approach to the standardization of classes and holds out great promise in creating a common core curriculum for transferring students. What about the future though?

Consider the following: A student rises from bed in the morning, eats breakfast, takes a shower, and settles down on the sofa. With laptop in hand, he or she logs into a real-time online class offered by the university two time-zones away. After completing the hour-and-a-half class, where the professor is actually interacting with the students, the student dresses and gets in the car for a drive across town. On the other side of town, the university is located in an office building. In a large conference room with a whiteboard, an instructor begins the calculus class. Remember that this is an entirely different university from the one attended earlier in the day. It's now lunchtime, and the student drives to work. At work from 1 p.m. to 5 p.m., the student is a half-time worker. At 5 o'clock, the student logs on to a MOOC with thousands of other students. Of course, the MOOC does not require the student to log in at a particular time of day—only to log in to take the class. At the end of each one-hour MOOC, there is a standardized multiple-choice test. The student completes this test with 90% accuracy and moves to evening instruction, which is at a local for-profit university. In the background and generally unnoticed by the student is a consolidating service that allows the student to take classes at multiple venues and have them recognized by either a certification program or a single diploma-granting university.

While this may seem far-fetched, think about what's happening in healthcare. For years, hospitals were considered the place where all types of medicine were delivered. Over time, specialty hospitals such as cancer centers, outpatient surgery, renal clinics, and ophthalmology hospitals evolved. These alternative venues have evolved for a very good reason—they provide services better than the general hospital! Simply, they do one thing, and they do it very well. Under the traditional model of higher education, it is assumed that one institution does everything, just like the traditional hospital. In reality, what's to stop a university from only doing one thing? This is a model that used to happen years ago when nursing colleges existed inside of hospitals. All they did was train nurses, and they trained them very well. At some point, all of these nursing colleges closed, and they became integrated into larger university systems.

In the example above, the first class may have been at the university where the student is actually based. Although the class is offered online, the student could have been in the room with other students. This university might be using telepresence, and the student actually has the option of being there in person or not. The second class, which was a math class, may be offered by a specialty program in math that teaches all of the math classes for the university and for many others. The program may teach math better than anyone else, and when the local university needs them, they can also participate in research projects. Mostly, however, they just teach math.

Notice that the student still has the opportunity to have a half-time job, in this case, in the middle of the day. The flexibility to be trained in multiple venues allows the student to be a productive member of the workforce. Contrast this with traditional education where essentially, a student disappears from the workforce for four to six years.

The third class, you may recall, is a MOOC, and once again this class is offered on enormous scale by a well-known university that specializes in the delivery of high-quality content to very large classes. If you consider the traditional model in large universities of having 500 students in a single class, why would 10,000 be any different? Teaching assistants could still hold tutoring sessions, but the university can now potentially eliminate the need for many of their very large lecture halls.

The fourth class of the day might be taught by one of our for-profit schools such as the University of Phoenix or Kaplan that generally do a very good job training working adults in MBAs or technical programs.

The key to this program is the ability for all of these programs to work together as a consolidated educational unit. One challenge for this kind of program is that traditionally universities like to control the quality of their students. Additionally, paying outside entities with precious funds seems contrary to the goals of the organization. Consider, though, an MBA program that's having problems finding and retaining faculty. What if the program could contract Accounting 101 to a MOOC provider? Since the MOOC is a large venture driven by economies of scale, it may be possible for the university to pay something on the order of $20 per student, and free up large lecture halls for other purposes that would significantly reduce the cost of delivering many of their core curriculum classes. Additionally, because the MOOC operates at a large scale, the producer can afford to become an excellent producer of content. Courses can become such effective, high-quality productions, that the traditional university should not even try to compete.

In a December 26, 2014, *New York Times* article entitled "Colleges Reinvent Classes to Keep More Students in Science,"[5] the author discusses new methods of teaching science to students so that attrition is dramatically diminished. Part of the strategy is to make the classes more interesting for a type of student very different from those in the past—one more attuned to the fast-changing world. Taking the article's concept a step further, when possible, why not hand over standard classes to companies that are very focused on making the experience as rich as possible? After all, we pay lots of money

---

[5] Pérez-Peña, Richard. "Colleges Reinvent Classes to Keep More Students in Science," *New York Times,* Dec. 26, 2014. http://www.nytimes.com/2014/12/27/us/college-science-classes-failure-rates-soar-go-back-to-drawing-board.htm

to content providers such as movie studios to craft messages in the most effective way possible. So why continue to play hit-and-miss with large classes of students that we through the general outsourcing of responsibilities to graduate assistants with no actual experience teaching? Once again though, this would require a significant change in attitudes at the university level.

A significant challenge to this type of change resides in the power of the university to convey a diploma. In many respects, the system is rigged so the change will not take place. Therefore, if anyone is waiting for this type of model to develop independently it may be a long wait. What will drive change to the model?

It's likely the change will happen at the employer level. A colleague was recently at a large company trying to convince them to send their employees to his MBA program for advanced training. In no uncertain terms, this large employer said, "We want our employees to learn skills, not earn degrees." Perhaps this is an indicator of how change will take place in higher education. Hypothetically, given this statement, our colleague and his institution only have a couple of options. The first option, of course, is to continue on their path and write this off as a single organization that has goals different from those of the rest of the world. This is a high-stakes gamble for an MBA program. As stated earlier in this chapter, more and more companies are becoming concerned about the amount of training they have to do before new, college-educated employees are productive.

If employers and students begin to favor certifications such as those offered to project managers and innovation professionals over degrees such as an MBA, then what other certifications might develop that are currently part of an MBA curriculum? Could an organization develop a certification in corporate finance, which is a very important element of any MBA program? There are new certifications in marketing, and would it be inconceivable that the American Society of CPAs offer MBA level certification? Alternatively, more progressive universities are already recognizing that working professionals may prefer a certificate in management from a highly regarded university to an MBA from a poorly regarded one.

So with this door open and universities offering more certification programs, how long will it be until there is a consolidator of certification programs? Could we then achieve a tipping point and move down to the four-year degrees? As mentioned earlier, there is a strong economic and operational incentive to outsource programs and courses that may or may not be profitable. An even better question is how long will it be until students and companies demand it? If several universities were to come together in creating a consortia and honoring each other's programs, then we might see these kinds of changes materialize.

The View From the Constituencies

Constituencies under this new paradigm would include:

- Traditional learners
- Adult learners
- Professors
- Administrators

- Employers
- Governments
- Parents
- Alumni

Traditional learners have seen the cost of a university education increase significantly over the last several years, while the ability to complete a program in four years erodes to something closer to six years. For a student and traditional learner, this is unacceptable. Under a new paradigm, traditional learners will see several possible improvements to the programs. These would include being able to be educated in the venue of their choice that best suits them, and by a better-caliber instructor. This could allow greater efficiency, which would bring down the cost of education and compress the time required to receive it.

Some learners are already operating under this new paradigm. Programs such as the University of Phoenix offer many graduate programs to working adults. The only part that is still missing is the portability of the courses they take. For example, if one program offers a class that is much higher quality at a lower cost than in the program they are in, all too often it's not an option to either take or transfer it. Should the paradigm shift so that these two lower the cost of education while improving the experience for the working adult?

Professors may appear to be the losers under the new paradigm. While prima fascia this could be true, it may actually be the opposite. Because professors were originally considered the content specialists and a significant number of professors do not actually enjoy teaching but are forced to do so by their contracts, they may find alternative outlets for expressing their knowledge and be able to get out of the classroom. In effect, this makes them consultants to content providers. A common student complaint about math classes is that they move too fast. Another is that they are not able to fully understand instructors of different ethnicities than themselves. Great mathematicians can inform great presenters and content providers, thus giving the mathematicians the opportunity to do what they really love, which is math, while outsourcing the actual teaching of the content to someone who may be better suited to reaching the audience. Additionally, there are companies who can help instructors with graphics and alternative presentation methods that may really excite young students. One question would be whether or not a professor then can earn a better living than they currently do. We believe that many professors, given the opportunity to be consultants while focusing on research, may find that they make more money than ever before.

Administrators can begin to focus on the management of the student and content as universities become more businesslike. A common complaint we hear from academics, including administrators, is that too many meetings are run by people who aren't qualified in the topic. For example, an English professor with little or no knowledge of human resources chairs a human resources committee. While the new paradigm may not do anything for English professors chairing HR committees, outsourcing certain classes will create a better opportunity to manage student careers instead of fellow employees.

Employers stand to gain significantly as well as the students. As mentioned numerous times in this chapter, employers have told us time and time again that the college graduates they hire may not actually have the skill sets that they need. Being forced to hire people who do not have the ability to do the job and having to take years to train them is a significant drain on the organization as well as society. When employers have the ability to pay for classes for their existing employees and choose the best certifications and classes from the best institutions, competition develops in a real-world setting. For society as a whole, this is a good.

Governments traditionally have been in the business of educating their citizens. In the United States, governments pay almost the entire cost of public K-12 programs. Why higher education became a private matter as a historical fact is beyond the scope of this chapter. In higher education, as with healthcare, the government has a significant interest in the outcome. Since the government in one way or another pays a significant part of the healthcare bill of the average American and in theory this leads to a healthier population who then works more and pays more in taxes, government-funded healthcare benefits society. In an efficient higher education system that is heavily funded by subsidized federal loans and grants, the government should be promoting the advancement of new models of education because a more educated population is more productive and contributes more to the tax base. Beyond that, more education tends to lead to more jobs, and more jobs tend to make for a better country. From a government perspective, the new paradigm makes a lot of sense.

Parents have a lot to do with the educational aspirations of their children. It has become almost cliché that parents want their children to do better than they did. Many times this is measured by educational attainment. A significant headwind the paradigm shift faces is the institutionalized belief that you should always send your child to the best school possible. Unfortunately, the best school possible is probably the most expensive school possible. There is strong evidence that the best thing that can be achieved by sending your child to the best school possible is related to the network that they develop with other smart kids from successful families. Whether the education is actually better is up for debate. From the other side, if some of the classes that your student can take are MOOCs that were developed and taught by professors from these top schools, then the student achieves a high-quality education at a much lower cost. There should be no reason that parents should be forced to sacrifice their retirement funds to send their children to a college that is more expensive than it needs to be. At the same time, every child deserves the best education they can possibly get.

Alumni probably suffer more than anyone from this change in paradigm. When you travel around certain parts of the country, you may find that affiliation with a certain university or college is one of the most important things in a person's life. You can see this with the tremendous turnout at football games for schools like Notre Dame and Brigham Young University. Some of this is the alumni network, and some of it is affiliated with things like religion and family tradition. There is a lot to be said for being an alumnus of certain universities or colleges, and it can be a lot of fun being part of that affinity group. The problem is that the world is changing and so might some of the traditions that come with being alumni of a prestigious university.

Conclusion

In our new world of higher education, a four-year degree once again takes four years to complete, and the value of an education (earned income over the cost) is improved. Students receive an education that is tailored to their individual needs instead of their being forced into a traditional system that has them move away from home and drop out of the world for four to six years. In the new world, they learn in a place of their choosing, whether that be in a dorm room, a homeroom, or a coffee shop. There are tremendous opportunities.

Most of the possibilities are driven by the capabilities created by new technology. The current model of higher education was developed during the time when students had to come to the ivory tower, the place where the smartest people reside, to be mentored before moving to the next stage of life. Remember this model was built at a time when education was a very good investment, and a good education was a great investment. It was also built during the time when a college degree was highly valued by society, and employers felt that the program was a rite of passage. In the new fast-paced world driven by results and credentials, this model may be coming to an end. Yes, there will always be the need for the university experience. Certain types of training should be done in person, but not necessarily all. Even a surgeon can be trained in a simulator these days. What is important for universities and other institutions of higher education to realize is that the world is changing, and now the ivory tower needs to come to the student. Once again, not in all cases but in those cases that make sense, the delivery of a highly efficient and effective educational program to all students throughout the world can be a very profitable proposition for universities. Thinking outside the box about divesting some of the massive infrastructure that most universities carry will be the trick. Universities can invest now in the support of MOOCs that they generate or that they honor within their own program. For example, even if a MOOC doesn't currently offer an exam grade at the end, why should this keep a professor from offering a written exam, holding a tutoring session, and offering credit for a class? In many cases this actually offers the best of both worlds: a great presenter and a great mentor.

The changes that need to take place to make this work are not insignificant. Universities will need to recognize that the world is changing. Accrediting organizations should allow universities to experiment with new methods of delivering content, including content that isn't necessarily even delivered by the university that gives the credit. Technology companies should begin to consolidate courses across universities. This means a leadership role by the technology community to both develop and direct these types of programs.

After spending the last four months interviewing employers, academics, and administrators, we see that there is a lot of frustration about the current system. We hope that this book encourages those in the higher ed community to think differently about the possibilities afforded by modern technology, great minds, and great students.

BRETT E. TRUSKO is on the faculty of Texas A&M University, Mount Sinai College of Medicine, and New York University. He is also the President and CEO of the International Association of Innovation Professionals (IAOIP) and the Editor-in-Chief of the *International Journal of Innovation Science* (IJIS). The IAOIP and IJIS advocate for the formalization of innovation and the creation of an international standard for innovation certification. He has a DBA in Business Administration and Technology Management and has over 30 years of experience including innovation, quality, strategy, informatics, operations, and administration. His focus throughout his career has been on harnessing human innovation to capture the potential of technology in the improvement of business.

42

Chapter 2
Tottering Ivory Towers

Chapter 2

Tottering Ivory Towers

By Stuart Butler

Board meetings of college trustees can be depressing affairs these days. Simply passing on rising costs—some of them externally imposed, others the harvest of bad or avaricious executive judgments—to compliant customers is rapidly becoming a thing of the past. Prospective students and their anxious parents are increasingly resistant to tuition hikes and crushing debt. Young Americans realize that a degree no longer ensures a full-time job related to their major; indeed, employer surveys indicate that more than half of America's graduates cannot find full-time work in their primary field of study. True, some majors, such as engineering, assure a good return on investment, but others, like psychology, do not. Meanwhile, the ability of colleges to mask the real-world benefits of their degrees is eroding fast thanks to scorecards from *U.S. News, Kiplinger's,* and *Forbes.* Families now incline to toss the glossy brochures and do the math.

Even more worrying and confusing to college presidents and trustees is the challenge coming from purveyors of online education products, from both for-profit companies and some of their own kind. In particular, the appearance of "massive open online courses" (MOOCs) over the past few years has thrown many of them for a loop. As others have warned, more such innovations are in the works.[1]

---

[1] Nathan Harden, "The End of the University as We Know It," *The American Interest,* January/February 2013.

Still, it's hard for most college leaders to believe that the "sage on a stage" business model truly could be doomed. It has lasted for more than 2,000 years, after all, with just a few minor modifications like PowerPoint, email, and online research. However, if today's college leaders—even at the Ivies—believe they can merely tweak their business models to carry them into the future, then they are in for an even more unpleasant surprise. They should ponder the still recent experience of the music industry, film and television, booksellers, and news media. If they did, they would soon recognize that the higher education industry is encountering a multi-pronged and existential threat composed of successive waves of disruptive innovation. This disruption will force top-to-bottom changes in the very concept of higher education and its relationship with the broader economy.

Change in an industry can be both rapid and brutal, especially when new technology is involved. A century ago, harness- and saddle-makers could tweak their business models all they liked, but they were flattened nevertheless by the automobile industry. Take the convulsions in the radio industry triggered by the invention of the transistor. From the 1930s to the 1950s the vacuum-tube radio was an expensive piece of furniture in the living rooms of middle-class homes throughout America and Western Europe. In the typical family, father controlled the programming, and his choice likely was some combination of sports, news, and big-band music. In England, where I was raised, we kids spent most evenings enduring the syrupy strains of Mantovani, Britain's rather lame answer to Glenn Miller.

But in 1955 Sony of Japan introduced the mass-produced battery transistor radio. It was cheap, plastic, and the sound was, well, pretty awful. But that didn't matter. It wasn't aimed at dad. It was marketed to teenagers, a customer base completely ignored by firms like RCA and the makers of high-quality vacuum-tube technology. Crackly sound was good enough for rock 'n' roll, especially if one listened to it under the bed covers rather than in the living room. But Sony didn't stop there. It steadily improved the technology while still focusing on its new listeners. Within a decade the transistor radio had been perfected into a direct competitor to RCA and the old technology, delivering similar quality at a fraction of the size and cost. That combination of comparable quality and sharply lower cost enabled the transistor radio to invade the living room market, crushing established industry leaders and transforming the family sound system.

Or think about the disruption of the newspaper industry. The old business model, essentially unchanged for 200 years, rested on three legs. The first of these involved a large capital investment in a network of quality journalists and news collectors, with papers like the *New York Times* or the *London Times* maintaining bureaus worldwide, feeding stories to their own mastheads and selling features to networks of regional papers. Smaller outlets couldn't possibly challenge such behemoths. The second leg was cross-subsidization of this costly news collection and feature writing through classified- and display- advertising, keeping copy prices down, circulation up, and advertisers happy. And third, in many markets the high-entry costs of starting a newspaper (large printing presses, distribution networks, and so on) often meant papers enjoyed a regional monopoly (or sometimes separate morning and afternoon papers), making overall industry economics even more stable.

Then the internet arrived. Three convulsions quickly followed. Suddenly breaking news in print became available 24/7 from a multitude of sources. True, the information on this airline crash or that African war was not of the same quality as a *New York Times* story, but for many it was good enough. There were words and pictures, and you didn't have to wait until tomorrow morning for them. Like the transistor, internet news appealed to new customers who were usually interested in good-enough news as long as it was cheap and immediate. And just like the transistor radio, as internet news improved in quality, it began to compete directly for traditional newspaper customers.

The second convulsion followed the appearance of new kinds of news intermediaries like the *Huffington Post.* These new ventures aggregated news put out by newspaper bureaus and hired their own young, low-paid journalists to package and customize that news and opinion for specific cadres of consumers. Tracking software and other technologies permitted such customization at little or no cost, but this was something most printed newspapers couldn't do.

Meanwhile, a third front opened up thanks to online advertising and free or low-cost information lists, such as Craigslist. These lists cut deep into the revenue source that had permitted newspaper cross-subsidization and hence profits.

The newspaper industry is still reeling from this triple whammy as shell-shocked newspaper barons scramble to find new business models that can withstand this new technology and upstart news suppliers. Like many industries facing such disruption, some newspapers have tried to incorporate the new technology to spruce up or protect their existing business model. For instance, the *New York Times* and many other prestige newspapers set up online versions of the paper with paywalls denying access to some content for non-paying readers. Interestingly, the strategies of some universities facing online competition have been similar. The university equivalent of the newspaper paywall strategy, pursued especially by prestige institutions like Harvard and Yale, has been to offer free glimpses of popular academic performers though a publicly available program, such as Harvard Extension's offering of Michael Sandel's famed course on justice, while maintaining tuition-based degrees.

The Paywall Strategy

Yet newspapers quickly discovered that the paywall strategy only works well if the content offers more value than regular news and opinion, such as one can find at the *Wall Street Journal* or the *Economist*. Many universities have copied that strategy, using a paywall for casual, non-student customers who want supplementary course content and feedback. They restrict the valuable branded degree credit only to those willing to pay big tuition bucks. Watching Sandel is free, but the cost of getting Harvard credit for his class is comparable to regular tuition.

Nevertheless, college presidents should note that the paywall strategy hasn't stopped U.S. newspaper revenues from plunging to half their 2000 levels nor has it kept large newspapers like the *Boston Globe* off the auction block. Other papers have shut down entirely. Even the venerable *Washington Post* survived for only a few years with cross-subsidies from the other profitable commercial ventures in its holding company. Today it's a side-project for Amazon's Jeff Bezos.

In practice, the strategy of trying to absorb competing services rarely does more than buy time. Experts on disruptive innovation, like Harvard Business School's Clay Christensen, point to typical patterns and experiences that should be dire warnings for university leaders hoping to ride out change.

One such pattern is that the entrepreneurs with new technologies and new business models typically aim first at customers who have been ignored or underserved by traditional industry leaders. That makes it easy for the current industry leaders to ignore them—a critical mistake—leaving the upstarts to occupy a sector of the market of little interest to industry leaders. Sony went after teenagers, who typically are not in the market for expensive electronic furniture or crystal-clear, concert-quality sound. Online news aggregators first aimed at busy multitaskers sitting at their computers, and at young people with distinct tastes and only casual interest in the news. Their targeted customer initially was not the lawyer in Brooklyn or in London who was interested in reading a three-part, prize-winning article on the Middle East or relaxing with the crossword.

The same has been true in higher education. Early versions of online courses appealed to students who could not easily maintain a regular schedule, or who needed more time to understand material. Major universities are beginning to introduce more blended online courses into their regular programs as a tweak to their offerings, but most see these as an added benefit for their traditional students rather than as tools to build completely new markets for nontraditional customers, such as part-timers or would-be students who simply cannot afford a traditional degree.

This attitude is reinforced by another common feature of the new products that will eventually disrupt an industry's primary market: Initially, they aren't very good. Sony's cheap, static-filled, and easily breakable plastic radios seemed safe to ignore. The Apple I, introduced in 1976, hardly seemed a harbinger of doom to the managers of IBM's mainframe monsters. So it is no surprise today to read college presidents denigrating MOOCs and the cheap, no-frills degrees being rolled out in Texas and Florida. You get what you pay for! Look at the huge non-completion rate for MOOCs! Online interaction can't replicate the true college experience! (Even if the tab for the latter runs in the tens of thousands of dollars.)

MOOC Refinements and Unbundling Full Service

Overlooked in this slough of disdain, however, is an important stage of disruptive innovation. Left alone in markets largely ignored by industry leaders, upstart innovators can refine their products and introduce new versions, steadily improving quality while retaining the price advantage and other features that make them attractive to underserved customers. It is that period of refinement that eventually produces the real giant-killers. New technology and its adaptation to markets proceeds in waves of innovation. The clunky Apple I sold just a couple hundred units, but the elegant Macintosh, introduced 20 years later, ransacked the computing industry.

That's why the shortcomings of MOOCs today should be of little comfort to the higher education establishment. The *New York Times* was indeed premature to declare 2012 to be "The Year of the MOOC," because the model is still in a feverish period of refinement and experimentation all over the world. For example, Britain's Open University—itself a pathbreaker launched in 1971 with a television and radio platform—has now created a MOOC called Futurelearn with university partners and non-university partners such as the renowned British Museum. France's École Polytechnique is offering MOOCs in French. Educators all over Africa and in Brazil see MOOCs as the teaching equivalent of telemedicine. These business model innovations allow a new technology to leapfrog over old technologies and business models, as the cellphone has done over the landline, making new communications networks widely available in the once telephone-starved countries of eastern Europe or Africa, or in the streets of Cairo.

The MOOC is evolving quickly. Coursera is among the MOOC providers exploring intriguing innovations such as peer grading to measure individual student performance at very low cost. Meanwhile, Udacity has started offering MOOCs for credit, as well as a complete online MOOC-based master's degree in partnership with the Georgia Institute of Technology, one of America's top technical schools, for less than $7,000. It is these second-wave and subsequent developments that will become the true Macintosh-style devastating threats to expensive, top-heavy traditional higher education and its business model.

Low-cost ventures of so-so quality also pose a potentially devastating threat by undermining cross-subsidies in a traditional business model. Website advertising and Craigslist were deadly to the economics of newspapers because experienced journalists and news bureaus need cross subsidies to survive, just as full-service hospitals do. The reason why getting a few stitches in the ER can cost a small fortune is that ER procedures make possible high-quality care in low-revenue generating areas such as pediatrics. That, in turn, is why the growth of walk-in clinics and other providers offering low prices for low-cost services is such a threat to big hospitals. The breakup of such cross-subsidized services is often referred to as "unbundling," and it is a worrying phenomenon for "full-service" providers in any industry. This is precisely what we are seeing in higher education.

As with hospitals and newspapers, bricks-and-mortar institutions of higher education are particularly vulnerable to unbundling. Universities are modular institutions, and lower-cost competitors can easily siphon off customers and revenue from individual modules. For instance, universities are partly a hotel and food-service industry, and partly sports and entertainment centers. They have invested heavily in buildings and services that package these elements together at essentially one price. But this makes them vulnerable to competitors that find much less expensive ways to provide discrete modules like housing or even basic first-year classes—or that simply shed costly facilities like libraries or student centers, as online colleges have done.

Indeed, the most challenging and decisive feature of unbundling and competition for the low-cost parts of the college bundle of services comes from the fact that the price of academic information is falling nearly to zero. Why pay a ton of money to sit with 300 other freshmen, listening to a Nobel Prize winner you will never actually meet on campus, when you have access to everything he has written, maybe even video versions of his lectures, free of charge on the internet? Johns Hopkins University professor Jakub Grygiel grumbles that such online courses lack the illuminating back and forth of the live seminar.[2] That was true just months ago, but it's fast becoming an exaggeration. Virtual class exchanges on Blackboard or GoToMeeting, or sometimes even Twitter, can be as stimulating as in-person seminars—and they come complete with links to citations and a record of the conversation that can be perused later.

But what about the social "college experience"? Well maybe that can be unbundled, too. Does undergraduate college have to last four years, or could the residential, networking, or sports elements occupy just part of the period of study at much less total cost? Britain's Open University has for years brought students on campus for just a few weeks each year. It retains a similar model today using online classes instead of its original televised courses. Yet it is number three in the UK for student satisfaction, tied with Oxford. Moreover, for many young people today online networking provides the relationship of choice for professional purposes, not just for social life. For them, Facebook, LinkedIn, and texting can be a more efficient and even more personal way of building and maintaining future career contacts than paying for a dorm or hanging out at a college gym.

The Role of Public Policy and Employers

While HBS's Christensen and others focus mainly on technological and business-model developments that lead to disruption, it's important not to overlook the importance of public policy as a spur or an obstacle to fundamental change in an

---

[2] Jakub Grygiel, "The MOOC Fraud," *The American Interest,* January/February 2014.

industry. Sometimes a law or regulatory decision can trigger dramatic change.

Consider in this light the U.S. Federal Communications Commission's 1976 Execunet decision that deregulated long-distance telephone service in the United States by ending AT&T's monopoly. That led to the invasion of the U.S. business and residential telephone market by firms that previously had been restricted to small markets. For instance, the Southern Pacific Railroad had maintained an extensive microwave communications system along its rights of way for its own benefit and for some private business lines. But regulation had prevented the company from using its internal network as the backbone for a new line of business offering telephone service. The FCC decision changed all that and allowed it, along with companies like MCI, to offer telephone service in direct competition with AT&T. The new company's name? Southern Pacific Railroad Internal Network Telecommunications—SPRINT. It has done pretty well.

Sweeping change in higher education is also being held back, at least temporarily, by regulation. The biggest impediment is accreditation. Portrayed as upholding quality standards, today the accreditation of colleges and universities is actually little more than a protectionist barrier benefitting existing institutions. Federal student loans are only available for accredited institutions. That means many new education ventures feel they must apply for accreditation, which can be an expensive, time-consuming, and uncertain process.

It is unlikely that today's colleges and universities will be able to hide behind accreditation for long, however. For one thing, there is growing interest in new ways of measuring the quality of a degree. The variety of scorecards now available, for instance, means students and their parents have much better and more granular measures of quality than accreditation provides. For another, employers are gradually making greater use of independent, competency-based measures and credentialed courses rather than relying on accredited degrees and credit hours (derided as "seat time" by its critics). Try getting a job in computer network management if you can't show which Microsoft Certified Systems Engineer courses you have passed. Meanwhile, Udacity is partnering with Google, AT&T, and other technology firms in an "Open Education Alliance" to provide top-level technical skills. Nevertheless, when it comes to alternatives to accreditation, the United States is generally playing catch-up with some other countries. In Britain, for instance, students can earn employer-union certified City & Guilds qualifications while studying at almost any institution, and there are standard competency measures in a variety of professional fields.

Federal action may be on the way. The Obama Administration is already encouraging colleges to seek approval for degree programs that are based on competency measures rather than credit hours. And legislation now circulating on Capitol Hill would allow states to create alternative forms of accreditation, possibly in conjunction with business groups, which would essentially break open the traditional system and undercut the power of traditional universities.

Big change will happen in America when employers start routinely recognizing alternatives to traditional degrees at traditional, accredited universities. That may not be too long in coming. Employers are increasingly frustrated with graduates who don't demonstrate the skills their transcripts suggest they have. In a *New York Times* interview, Google's senior vice president for people operations, Laszlo Bock, admitted that transcripts, test scores, and even degrees are less useful than other data as predictors of employee success.[3] In this environment, an industry-led move to create a more dependable measure of knowledge and ability than a transcript will become increasingly attractive.

Anticipated Responses

When the process of innovation moves in from the edges of higher education and begins to disrupt the business models of leading public and private institutions, what will higher education look like? Considering the pattern in other industries, how should existing colleges and universities respond to the threat to their survival? Can they respond?

The critical lesson from the transformation of other industries is that it is likely to be a disastrous mistake to assume you can just tweak an existing business model and be all right. That can work only for a while. When online airline booking was new but technically challenging to use, travel agents adopted it to make their jobs easier and more profitable. But once it became user-friendly it destroyed their jobs, more or less the same way that essentially free information about stocks and bonds destroyed the traditional careers of stock dealers and bond salesmen.

In education even the most established and financially secure institutions will have to revamp their business models to

---

[3] Adam Bryant, "In Head-Hunting, Big Data May Not Be Such a Big Deal," *New York Times,* June 19, 2013.

survive. Yale, MIT, and Harvard, among the high-status schools, do seem to be taking online education innovations seriously, experimenting with special course offerings through extension programs and lower-cost degrees such as accelerated executive MBAs. Some are even trying to set the pace by developing MOOCs of their own, such as the edX venture launched in 2012 by MIT and Harvard and now offered to other schools.

But it is unlikely to be smooth sailing even for them. Innovative deans and college presidents often face tenured faculty who resist change. Moreover, they have a valuable and costly brand to protect, and elites who offer lower-end goods and services do court danger. Top clothiers like Nordstrom had to be careful about the perception of their valuable brand when they opened discount stores. Likewise, the more elite universities attach their brand names to less expensive, second-tier products, the more they endanger their brand and invite their primary customers to question the extra value they get for their $40,000 in annual tuition. They risk unbundling themselves from their own prestige.

What of the rest? Where value-for-money, rather than a tony brand, is the competitive edge, colleges are more inclined to consider partnerships designed to gain an edge. For instance, several U.S. state university systems, including the State University of New York and the University System of Georgia, have teamed up with MOOC giant Coursera to offer online courses and test out new business models and teaching methods. Some international partnerships are reshaping graduate education in professional fields. The for-profit Kaplan University maintains a facility in Singapore, for instance, with academic partners all over the world, from Murdoch University in

Australia to several universities in Britain. And Arizona State University hit the headlines recently thanks to its path-breaking agreement with Starbucks, allowing the coffeehouse giant to offer tuition-free degrees. These arrangements help established-universities reduce costs while building up a more sophisticated online presence that could eventually become a core feature of their business models.

Some of the second- and lower-tier institutions are willing to change their brands in pace-setting ways. Take Southern New Hampshire University, once just a small, typical private New England college. It now offers several broad paths for a degree: at its original 300-acre wooded campus in Manchester; at regional centers in New England; or predominantly online, where students can opt for professional certification as well as degrees. Always on the cutting edge, it has just launched a nationally available, self-paced $10,000 competency-based degree program through a new venture called College for America. It's designed for working adults and their employers and will center on project-based learning, rather than traditional lectures and credit hours, in conjunction with partner employers, including McDonald's, Anthem Blue Cross, and Gulf.

Nathan Harden predicted not so long ago that thanks to the online revolution, roughly half the nation's colleges and universities will cease to exist within the next 50 years.[4] He's probably right, though many may end in mergers. But I suspect the pace of change will be much faster than that. Harden is likely right, too, about many of the structural changes we can expect, given the history of other industries. He sees

---

[4] Nathan Harden, "The End of the University as We Know It," *The American Interest,* January/February 2013.

a war for survival, as we've seen in the newspaper industry, with the "bottom feeders," as he somewhat disparagingly calls them, disappearing entirely or turning into vocational institutes.

But while most low-quality degree factories undoubtedly will go out of business as full colleges, a likely scenario is that the general unbundling of educational services will lead to a new array of institutions delivering degrees and degree equivalents. Some will be aimed at students seeking solid credentials at low cost with no frills; others will provide a more face-to-face experience than is typically the case today with online education. In other words, the models will collapse on one another to some extent from both directions.

No-Frills Options

The no-frills option will be an enormous boon to young people from poorer neighborhoods who need college-level skills to have any chance of upward economic mobility. These young Americans are ill-served by today's costly and inflexible system. What they need and want is a combination of self-paced, online learning, supplemented by talented teachers rather than occasional sightings of big names who would rather be doing research. No-frills ventures are more likely to have "campus" classes taught after hours in high schools or in Skype tutorials at home, with a standard competency-based credential accepted by employers and that accurately measures student skills. And they will likely cost a lot less than today's traditional degrees, as well as being as good and in many instances better and more marketable than them. The $10,000 degree probably is just the beginning of a sharp price reduction that will do much to spur upward mobility for millions of young people born into lower-income families.

An unbundled education does not have to be provided the same way or in the same location each year. Education innovator Salman Khan of Khan Academy speaks in *The One World Schoolhouse* of future students transferring frequently, getting pieces of the overall package at different institutions. Given the concerns of both students and employers about the real-world value of a college education, an integral part of gaining a useful credential can and should be experienced, he believes, as an intern or apprentice in work settings. Southern New Hampshire University recognizes this with College for America. The University of Southern California now emphasizes serious career planning and student experience with partners in the working world as essential for marketing the value of its degree. More formal apprenticeships are much less common in the United States than in Europe, but with companies stressing the importance of an appropriately skilled and trained workforce as the most important factor in their location decisions, they may begin to take firmer root here. In Charlotte, North Carolina, for instance, the German company Siemens and other firms partner with Central Piedmont Community College to offer paid apprenticeships and associate degrees with a guaranteed job after graduation. Expect many more developments like these.

Price-Discrimination vs. Cross-Subsidies

To survive in this rapidly changing world, existing institutions will have to do two things well. First, just like newspapers establishing paywalls or airlines selling seats at different prices to different customers, they will have to learn how to "price discriminate" rather than depend on cross-subsidies to maintain the elite and expensive parts of their brand. Not everyone wants to rub shoulders with top professors in tutorials. Many would gladly do the bulk of courses online. Some students want a credential as quickly and cheaply as possible. But others are willing to pay more for a high level of interaction, just as some people pay more for "concierge" physicians who are available outside of regular hours and spend more time with patients. They don't all need to pay the same tuition or have access to the same level and range of services, any more than people flying from New York to Paris in the same plane pay the same or get the same service or seat size.

Second, they will have to determine their true competitive advantage. Is it a beautiful campus? Is it small seminars with world-class academics? Future professional contacts? Or is it good quality classes at a low price? They will need to perfect and build on that advantage, and let someone else deliver other parts of the total higher education package. This means many colleges must accept that much basic course content will be delivered by other providers for free or nearly for free. We'll see a steady increase in basic courses provided less expensively and closer to home by community colleges and new ventures, often in formal partnership with universities and perhaps some businesses. Expect the equivalent of intramural or intervarsity sports to be organized by local high schools. And expect the distinction between college degrees and employer-sponsored credentialing to blur.

As a result, many of today's universities may end up providing only a couple of years of higher-level courses themselves. Indeed, the degree of the future is likely to become a customized collection of educational experiences and credentialed courses with many of today's colleges and universities becoming managers of a range of courses and experiences. The value of the college's brand, and the prices it can charge, will depend on how well it can assemble a package of in-house and contracted-out courses and services customized for each student—and on the overall quality of that package.

Some American university leaders will try to navigate these fraught times with a few tweaks here, a few layoffs there, and perhaps extra PowerPoint classes for the faculty. They will fail. Some will make concessions, using new technology for add-on services, while trying to build a moat around the traditional business model. They will also court failure. The ones who succeed truly will have learned the lessons of survivors in the consumer electronic, newspaper, and other industries facing the existential threat of disruptive innovation.

||||||||||||||||||||||||||||||||||||||||||||||||||||||||||||||||||||||||||||||||||||||||||||||||||||||||||||||||||||||||||||||||||||||||||||||||

STUART BUTLER is a senior fellow at the Brookings Institution in Washington, D.C. This article first appeared in The American Interest, September/October 2014 issue, and is reprinted with permission.

64

Chapter 3

The Future and Present Challenges of Higher Education

Chapter 3

An Ongoing Journey— Technology Trends for 2015 and Beyond

By Dr. Alan R. Shark

The Digital Revolution continues to grow at a rapid, exponential pace with each new advance quickly building upon the last. Information technology in particular serves as a powerful enabler that empowers people in ways that few could have contemplated just a few short years ago. Each day we become numbed with rather staggering future predictions, such as internet traffic will pass the zettabyte range by the year 2018, and also by 2018, global Internet traffic will be 64 times the entire volume of the internet in 2005. Similarly, by 2018, the gigabyte equivalent of all movies ever made will cross the Internet every three minutes.[1] Such examples are becoming as profound as they are impossible to visualize. If anyone needed convincing that the *Internet of Everything* had arrived, 2013 was the year when we realized that there were more mobile devices in the U.S. than people. Data communications surpassed voice, and machines are talking to one another almost as much as humans talk to one another. Clearly the Internet of Everything is now, even though it is still growing in size and scope. No institution,

---

[1] http://www.cisco.com/web/about/ac79/docs/IoE/IoE-VAS_Public-Sector_Top-10-Insights.pdf

especially higher education can escape its grasp. Some will view current events with fear and worry, while others will marvel about the possibilities and opportunities.

Traditional schools of higher education have withstood the tests of time, exercising complete control over when students are admitted and under what circumstances, when and how students graduate, when and how faculty receive tenure, and what degree programs are offered when. Perhaps nowhere else in modern society has such an institution been able to resist change while simultaneously promoting its stability as a cherished virtue. Higher educations' historical mission hasn't changed very much for the past few hundred years, but we are beginning to see signs that the digital revolution is helping to change higher education in many important ways.

It is interesting to note that some of the great digital innovators we have come to know went to college only to become dropouts. They were great nontraditional learners and have

always been strong supporters of higher education—but in their own way. They advanced beyond the confines of traditional higher education requirements. This list includes Bill Gates and Paul Allen, Microsoft; Steve Jobs, Apple; Michael Dell, Dell Computer; Larry Ellison, Oracle; and Mark Zuckerberg, Facebook, all of whom went on to become billionaires. Perhaps common to each was the frustration of wanting to move ahead of a curriculum that appeared to them as an obstacle instead of a launching pad. To be fair, these individuals are the exceptions, as hundreds of thousands of college graduates owe much credit to their positive college experiences for furthering their careers. If anything can be learned from this phenomenon it is that most students have different and individual learning needs that vary with time and circumstance. What is also different in contemporary society from just a few dozen years ago is the abundance of nontraditional learning opportunities that have flourished in the new digital age. Colleges and universities are now facing powerful winds of change, and they will either change or be changed—or perhaps, both.

Well before the term the *Internet of Things* (IoE) was coined and became popular, the internet was growing at a phenomenal pace leading to a more "connected society," which has been accelerated further by the advances in mobile devices. What began as a digital *evolution* in higher education has accelerated into nothing short of the beginning of a *revolution*. While higher education has surely taken advantage of many new technologies—albeit slowly, the cost and value of higher education has come into question. Whether one views investing in new technologies as a luxury or a necessity, questions remain regarding what might the future look like, and as importantly, how does it come about?

There are essentially five major categories where technology will continue to make an even greater impact in the years ahead. They are: 1) the learning environment, 2) the mobility factor, 3) research, information, and collaboration, 4) the "administration of things and people," and finally, 5) lifelong learning.

The Learning Environment

The physical structures of higher learning haven't changed much over time until recently. Some of the changes are visible, while others are not something one can see. In 2008, many faculty would have been happy to ban wi-fi access in college hallways, lounges, and in particular, classrooms. They viewed wireless connections to the Internet as an intrusion, because students could surf the web while in class and thus pay little attention to what was going on in class. While a few institutions of higher learning created "no wi-fi" or "no mobile

device" zones, the overwhelming majority are on their third or fourth generation of expanded and more powerful wi-fi options throughout the campus. Many faculty today encourage students to search the Internet for certain things even in the classroom, and they include such activity as part of class participation and interaction.

Many traditional classrooms have been converted into multimedia rooms, where giant video screens adorn the walls. Some rooms are equipped with a large screen and a special pen that allows faculty to draw over any screen display or simply write notes or equations. In other words, this relatively new option is like having a digital whiteboard for all to see, share, and perhaps save for future reference. This same smart-room technology provides the option of having students display what is on their own mobile devices. A student can share a presentation or even a website without leaving his or her seat. Faculty who teach remotely to a smart classroom can see and hear an entire class in high-definition video and sound as if they were actually physically present. While sound is always on, when a student presses a small microphone on a desk, the cameras are pre-programed to automatically zoom into focus on that student, which enables the professor to immediately identify who is speaking.

In many instances, today's traditional lecture is often supplemented by video clips such as those found on YouTube, TED Talks, and NatGeo, or with other web offerings explored as a group. In addition to or replacing their traditional written papers, students develop digital content and deliver presentations as individuals or as a group using PowerPoint, Prezi, or other presentation programs. Students can share their information and projects through collaboration programs, many of which are free to them. Students are encouraged to become digital explorers and to be more than consumers of information by creating information, too.

The *Internet of Things* is a term that describes how our society has become so interconnected both nationally and globally. Students sitting in a classroom in Newark, New Jersey can view in real time the data feeds of flood gauges on the Mississippi River or any other body of water. They can view live video feeds from all over the world, which might include guest lecturers in another city or country. Students looking at a website containing live data of a flu or other virus outbreak can take raw data and copy and paste it onto a cloud-based geographic information system (GIS) to better visualize the information and trends on a dynamic map. This type of activity brings data to life and greatly enhances a student's ability to digest vast amounts of data and better comprehend the information that could lead to better planning and analysis. This is another way of saying that technology can bring data to life! Thousands of video cameras are strewn around cities and inside buildings. They can provide free access to view what's going on day or night to just about anyone with a smart device or computer. Someone in Rome can watch a live feed of panda bears at the Smithsonian National Zoo in Washington, D.C. This is but another way we can all be observers of life as it unfolds and yet, still be able to provide content on our own.

YouTube has emerged as the video diary of life for millions of people—300 hours of video, coming from 71 countries and in 61 languages, is loaded onto YouTube every hour.[2]

The classroom learning environment involves both students and faculty. Lectures can be recorded and offered on demand. Faculty can foster greater student interaction by providing students with the ability to take quick polls on concepts, ideas, and perhaps short quizzes that provide instant feedback on a screen for all to see. This can be accomplished through the use of instant response devices sometimes called "clickers," or through the use of smartphones using special apps that ultimately provide an option for students to weigh in on issues and opinions and see how their responses compare to the group's.

Schools of higher learning are taking advantage of both synchronous and asynchronous (and hybrid) learning programs. Such programs are made possible through the use of advanced technologies and learning management systems (LMS). LMS systems like Blackboard or Moodle provide, among many things, a portal for posting papers, assignments, articles, videos, websites, and other types of content, such as course wikis and student grades. LMS systems also authenticate users and serve as a video and multi-media portal that offer almost unlimited resources to students. The digital revolution has made smart classrooms ever smarter, and there is much more to come. Already they have become more comfortable with improved high-tech lighting, dramatically improved connectivity including wireless access, larger display screens, clicker/polling device systems, and the ability to tap

---

[2] http://www.youtube.com/yt/press/statistics.html

into unlimited resources from around the globe. Some rooms contain cluster seating that is designed to encourage greater collaboration.

Students now enjoy feature-rich tablets and lightweight laptops or two-in-one devices. As long as there is reliable broadband, they can be connected to their fellow students as well as a college or university from almost anywhere.

As learning management systems (LMS) have become more sophisticated, they can measure a student's progress at any time. For example, they can let the professor know how many times a student was online and the duration and frequency of checking in with the class.

Libraries

Any discussion of the learning environment must also include the campus library. While many school libraries look the same as they did for the past few hundred years, there is a marked difference in the services they now provide. Surely libraries suffer from a lack of financial resources that limit what they can do and make it difficult for them to maintain enough expert staff. Yet despite budget limitations, libraries have steadfastly transformed themselves into rather exciting digital gateways. The Association of College & Research Libraries identified one unifying theme in its *2014 Top Trends in Academic Libraries* report, and that is "deeper collaboration" with the rest of the university and outside community. The top trends include data, device-neutral digital services, and evolving openness in higher education, student-success initiatives, competency-based learning, altmetrics, and digital humanities.[3] Libraries of the future will continue to offer a place to meet and work in solitude or work in a collaborative setting with ample broadband connectivity, both wired and wireless. Most will enhance their expertise and digital resources to

SOURCE: RUTGERS UNIVERSITY

---

[3] Association of College & Research Libraries, 2014 http://oai.wsu.edu/teaching_resources/resources.html

better serve the expanding needs of students, faculty, and the larger community. Expensive-to-maintain services that once resided in the library will increasingly move toward more economical and feature-rich cloud-based services. Library staff will be not only curators of information; they will serve as digital guides and collaborators.

New Technologies

New technologies will be added to the learning environment that will make learning and experimentation much more exciting and rewarding. One example is 3D printers, which have moved quickly from being a novelty invention in search of a market to an estimated $16 billion-plus industry by 2018.[4] Once limited to producing plastic reproductions of jewelry, the 3D printer now produces materials ranging from precious metals to human cartilage. One amazing example occurred when the International Space Station, in need of a specialized part, was

---

[4] http://oai.wsu.edu/teaching_resources/resources.html

able to produce it about 250 miles above Earth using an on-board 3D printer that received specifications and instructions that traveled some 17,000 miles per hour to reach it.

Today 3D printer models are available from retail outlets such as Office Depot, Amazon, and Best Buy. This type of device can be an excellent way of creating and duplicating objects relating to industrial design—especially transportation, printed organs in the medical field, industrial and consumer product-prototype design, environmental design—especially wind-driven power devices and solar-power panel design. 3D printers allow students to experience hands-on design without having to travel to an industrial lab that could be hundreds, if not thousands, of miles away. This technology provides the opportunity to experiment with exotic materials and new designs.

The next breakthrough in technology that also can enhance learning experiences will come in the form of wearable devices. Examples are smart glasses and visual headsets. Google Glass was considered a breakthrough when it first appeared in 2013 as a hands-free device that provided key information from a mobile device to a special eyepiece. After much publicity, it was shelved in 2015 for further development.

While Google Glass may be back in the planning stages, other companies, such as Microsoft, promise to address the need to better visualize objects and data. HoloLens is designed to work with the new Microsoft Windows operating system that will provide augmented-reality applications.[5] This device will be different in that the user can read data right on the lens,

---

[5] http://www.polygon.com/2015/1/21/7867641/windows-holographic-is-the-next-era-of-windows

and the unit contains immersive sound as well as a host of sensors. The main advantage of this technology is applied augmented reality. Augmented reality allows a user to see maps, pictures, and diagrams while also having visual data superimposed. Once in the market, students and faculty will be able to see, share, and explore things as never before.[6]

As the "wearables" market grows, there will be other manufacturers who will develop visual headsets similar to HoloLens and Google Glass. Other wearable devices include watches, many of which are on the market now, and operate either as a standalone device or in tandem to a smart device. The standalone type is primarily used to provide basic health metrics including sleep patterns, heart-rate, distance walked, skin temperature, and more. The tandem devices allow the user to recall data instantly without having to take out a mobile

[6]http://www.forbes.com/sites/insertcoin/2015/01/25/could-microsofts-hololens-be-the-real-deal/

device. They also are designed to provide health metrics to a computer and/ or a doctor. According to Juniper Research, there will be 770 million biometric apps by 2019.[7]

The Internet of Everything is comprised of millions of devices that are connected to each other. The number of devices is growing exponentially, and the growth of sensors everywhere provides the opportunity to tap into a wealth of raw data that can lead to expanded research opportunities. The learning environment will forever be changed by the many advances in technology as the class of 2020 will surely enjoy many exciting opportunities to learn, experience, and create.

The Mobility Factor

Everyday an average of 3.5 million smartphones are purchased.[8] According to consulting firm Gartner, there will be 4.9 billion connected things in 2015—up 30% from last year.[9] Data use in America can be described as taking 247 trips around the world every minute.[10] It is expected that video will represent 65% of mobile traffic by 2019.[11] Today 97% of households have mobile phones, and 15% of the population are said to own tablets.[12] The concept of place has changed

---

[7] http://www.juniperresearch.com/research/human-interface-biometric-devices

[8] http://www.ctia.org/resource-library/facts-and-infographics/archive/infographic-1.3-billion-smartphones-sold-worldwide-in-2014

[9] http://www.gartner.com/newsroom/id/2970017

[10] http://www.ctia.org/resource-library/facts-and-infographics/archive/infographic-americans'-data-usage-equals-247-trips-around-the-world-every-minute

[11] https://www.abiresearch.com/market-research/service/4g/

[12] http://www.ctia.org

significantly in the past decade as the mobility factor continues to transform our business and learning environments. Globally, IBM has over 430,000 employees, with approximately 40% working out of their residential home offices. Today's student is not always fresh out of high school. They now come in all ages, from many places, both urban and rural. Some return to college to develop new skills leading to new employment opportunities, others are looking to excel in their current positions. In recent years, the percentage increase in the number of students age 25 and over has been larger than the percentage increase in the number of younger students.[13] Many in the military assigned to various posts around the world are actively pursuing higher education too. Given the proliferation of broadband and distance learning options, students of just about any age or occupation can, from any location, sign up for a degree program at a college or university. Today's colleges and universities are realizing the growing interest in distance or online learning. In fact there has been a 96% increase in online courses in the past five years.[14]

Thanks to improvements and the growth of broadband, asynchronous online learning systems have greatly improved. Students can untether themselves from an office phone or speaker phone and listen to a class or an instructor's lecture. Today's technology permits students to use their tablets to both see and hear their online classmates and instructors. They can view online assignments, ask questions, view videos and readings, and track their progress at

---

[13] http://nces.ed.gov/fastfacts/display.asp?id=98

[14] http://campustechnology.com/articles/2013/06/24/report-students-taking-online-courses-jumps-96-percent-over-5-years.aspx

any time. Telepresence technology allows participants at various locations to see and hear one another as if they were in the same location in one another's virtual presence. This technology is excellent for learning, interviewing guests, or visiting experts and speakers. Video platforms like WebEx, Go-To-Meetings, Adobe Connect, Polycom, LifeSize, are just a few of the more popular video services and platforms used by higher education. Some of the platforms are web-based thus allowing for viewing multi-media, PowerPoint presentations, and live or recoded lectures in high-definition video and sound. Using mobile devices such as tablets, students can conduct and record interviews, check out environmental issues in the field, conduct surveys, and do other forms of research. Sensors that are tapped into the Internet of Everything, can be used to gather and share data. Students can be almost anywhere using their mobile devices to access digital libraries and references located in their home or school or even the Library of Congress. The new mobile order is here, where aside from a near insatiable demand for mobile growth

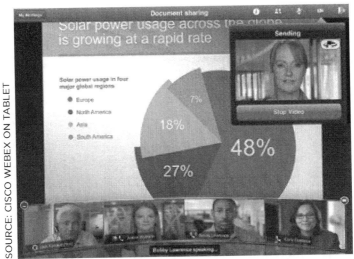

SOURCE: CISCO WEBEX ON TABLET

we will see a rise in software platforms and apps as well as newer and faster speeds and capacity.[15]

Students and faculty can now be highly interconnected even though they can be physically separated. Mobility offers higher education a whole new set of choices and delivery systems that maximize learning, research, and collaboration.

Research, Information & Collaboration

The digital revolution in higher education lends itself particularly well to research, information, and collaboration opportunities. The main driver for collaboration is social media through peer-to-peer groups, professional groups such as Linkedin, Twitter, Facebook, and at times, YouTube. Each research discipline vies for their respective affinity group's attention and participation. Collaboration has become more than a buzzword in academia as faculty and researchers can communicate instantaneously across the digital landscape. It's no longer unusual for a researcher in Prague to reach out to someone in Brooklyn to write a chapter or coauthor a study. Documents can be shared, stored, and marked up with each collaborator's signature. Video meetings now defy time zones and cultures. Mobile devices are used to assist with interviews and can be used to catalog items and behaviors being observed. In regards to items, mobile devices using bar codes or quick-response (QR) codes can track and store items, sending them when appropriate to a database at another location. Behaviors can be observed using mobile-device cameras whose output can also be stored and cataloged.

---

[15] https://www.cisco.com/web/about/ac79/docs/sp/New-Mobile-World-Order.pdf

Good research requires good peer review opportunities and other publishing opportunities, hence the rise of e-books and e-journals. We now have e-reader and e-books, leading to greater opportunities to publish data. Students benefit by having the option to purchase e-books, which are generally more affordable than traditional paper books. Printed encyclopedias have long since been replaced by powerful search engines and websites such as Wikipedia and Wolfram Alpha. Within the last five years federal agency websites have provided troves of information and data that is instantly available for research activities.[16] Local and state governments are also publishing data and creating user-friendly data sets on a routine basis. Cities such as Chicago, Philadelphia, New York, San Francisco, Miami-Dade County, and Montgomery County all have open data programs with websites showing newly published data. While much of the open data movement was initially inspired with the goal of helping to restore public trust through greater transparency, there is a growing recognition that data can help in making better and more informed decisions. Now, students and faculty have a growing resource of information that can help generate new research opportunities leading to practical solutions for difficult problems. Instead of merely reading textbooks, now students can experience things instantly bringing subject matter to life. Having 3D display will become common; sensors will connect to many new sources of data to explore and analyze. Mobile devices can be used to collect information and data that can be shared. Perhaps, statistical standards we now use for declaring accuracy will likely be increased because larger samples can be generated far more easily.

---

[16] http://data.gov

Administration of Things and People

Technology initially was relied upon to automate routine administrative practices. It made complete sense to automate check writing, accounting, and record keeping. Pre-internet voice-response systems allowed some students to register for classes using a touch-tone phone. Today faculty, students, and administrators have smart IDs that provide access to classrooms and other areas that can be centrally controlled and monitored for authorized access. Smart buildings have lights that turn off when they sense there is no activity. This category would also include smart thermostats and sensors that measure energy usage at any given time. Print management systems have replaced the need for personal printers, saving institutions millions of dollars in paper and maintenance costs. Online student registration saves both time and money and provides immediate course inventory controls. While external websites provide critical information on every aspect of college and faculty life, internal sites keep faculty administrators better informed of meetings, calendars, and important documents. Learning management systems link everything together that enable administrators to better know and understand what is happening at any moment in time on

the campus. Schools encourage the use of apps to stay in-formed and to be able to report things as they see them.

Campus safety has always been a concern regardless of loca-tion. The Internet of Everything provides the opportunity to link security cameras everywhere and specialized software will monitor various video feeds looking for anomalies that, if detected, will set off alarms. Most campuses today have emer-gency broadcast systems that can alert students to any type of emergency by sending a message directly to their mobile device. Sensors deployed in key areas are designed to detect fire/smoke or CO_2 levels. Some institutions are able to moni-tor plant operations, perimeter movements, and even flood-ing conditions. Smart meters can handle parking and regulate by demand and time of day. Drones, both tethered and unte-thered, will be used to monitor crowds and incidents in coor-dination with local authorities.

Finally, parents, who in one way or another pay for their sons and daughters to go to college, might soon have access to an app called "Class 120." This app is being tried by a few col-leges and is designed to alert parents when their kids skip or miss classes.

Lifelong Learning

When a student graduates with a college degree, it is a reflec-tion of past work and commitment. It is essentially a terminal degree in that there are no further requirements or obliga-tions. To the extent that a graduate chooses a profession or vocation, any advanced training is usually out of the hands of colleges and universities. Many professions today require a certification of some sort that measures proficiencies. More-over, certifications, unlike a college degree, usually require re-certification every few years. Given the complexity of chang-ing workforce requirements, it is reasonable to assume that there will be an increased need for lifelong learning. The digi-tal revolution offers multiple pathways toward lifelong learn-ing for professional development as well as for the pleasure of learning new skills or subject matter at an individual pace. Many educational offerings can be administered completely online or in a combination of onsite and offsite instruction. Nonprofit associations have been quick to embrace profes-sional certifications, as traditional colleges focused primarily on the college degree. Thus competition for lifelong learners will become fierce. Tablets will replace most books as we know them, and tests can be taken online or in an online proc-tored session.

Massive open online courses (MOOC) were first introduced in 2008, and by 2013 there were over 1 million students who had been enrolled in a MOOC. There have been studies that show that a very small percentage actually complete a MOOC.[17] While both growth and attention have waned, the concept is still very valid.[18] Perhaps too massive and too open, with some refinements, and scaling back the hype, they might well continue to fill a need for lifelong learners.[19] The future of lifelong learning is quite bright.[20] This has al-

---

[17] http://moocnewsandreviews.com/what-do-we-know-about-mooc-students-so-far/

[18] http://www.technologyreview.com/review/533406/what-are-moocs-good-for/

[19] http://www.nytimes.com/2014/11/02/education/edlife/demystify-ing-the-mooc.html?ref=topics&_r=0

[20] http://gettingsmart.com/2014/10/infographic-future-lifelong-learning/

lowed some schools to experiment with something called "badging," which can be defined as a method by which a student's activities and achievements can be measured outside of the traditional course framework.

Lifelong learning, as it turns out, has many different meanings. Many adults with more time on their hands are perhaps more interested in learning something than taking an actual course. The Discovery Channel, National Geographic, TED Talks, or even WebMD, and other informational sites are all competing for one's time and providing information. Corporations are viewing education at all level as a great place to invest. Some are predicting private investment in technology in higher education to be over $2 billion in 2015.[21] This number does not even begin to take into account companies that produce and sell software and hardware. And companies, seeing certain weaknesses in the traditional higher education marketplace, are moving into this environment by developing programs of their own.

The Internet of Things will enhance the collegiate college and university ecosystem as the focus will shift towards connecting people to people as well as device to device. Perhaps the greatest change moving forward will involve the concept of place. The Internet of Everything implies ubiquitous connectivity among humans and machines. Learning environments can and will be everywhere from 39,000 feet above ground aboard an airliner, to a ship at sea, to a tablet on a beach, or in a home office; it will matter less and less where a program originates. Research and collaboration will accelerate across the globe, and the administrative functions will shift from a focus on the

---

[21] http://www.geekwire.com/2015/can-count-2-billion-education-technology-investment-hits-new-record/

physical plant toward coordination and applied-use of technology-support services. The need for higher learning will never go away—but some tradition-bound institutions may no longer be around.

||||||||||||||||||||||||||||||||||||||||||||||||||||||||||||||||||||||||||||||||||||||||||||||||||||||||||||||||||||||||||||||||||||||||||||||||||||||||||||

DR. ALAN R. SHARK is the Executive Director and CEO of Public Technology Institute (PTI). Dr. Shark is a noted thought-leader, authors and sought-after speaker focusing on mobile and e-government, technology trends in government, as well as thought-leadership professional development issues for IT executives and public managers. He also serves an associate professor of practice at Rutgers University School of Public Affairs & Administration where he teaches a masters level course on technology and public administration, and also serves as the Director for The Center for Technology Leadership. He is the author of *Seven Trends that will Transform Local Government through Technology,* and is editor of the book *Smarter Cities for a Bright & Sustainable Future: A Global Perspective.*

He is the recipient of the prestigious 2012 National Technology Champion Award from the National Association of State Chief Information Officers and is a Fellow of the National Academy for Public Administration.

Chapter 4
A View from the Faculty

Chapter 4

A View From the Faculty

By Dr. Lance Ford and Mary Schlegelmilch

The integration of technology into the teaching and learning environments within higher education institutions is vital. We have not witnessed a transformation such as the digital age within higher education since the industrial revolution. Soliciting the input of faculty who have integrated technology into their teaching enables professors to continually reflect and adjust their own teaching styles to address the growing demands of their students.

Faculty are subject-matter experts in their respective fields, and traditionally courses have been lecture based—professors impart their knowledge to students through class-period-long recitations of their knowledge while students take notes. The digital age brings instant availability and access to technology, which is shifting today's students' attitudes about how they want to engage and design their learning processes. This student demand, as well as instructors' identifying the need to further engage students in the learning process, are leading the way to transforming and integrating technology into the classroom.

Throughout this chapter, we will highlight the experiences of faculty members from a variety of institutions who have adopted and invited the digital age into their learning environments. As we proposed writing this chapter, we asked professors from various institutions for their assistance and insights. It is their stories we share as case studies.

Faculty members approach the implementation of technology from various experience and perception levels (Rogers, 1995) thus identified in various adoption categories: innovators, early adopters, early majority, late majority, and laggards. Often faculty look toward the integration of technology to help solve an issue within their course or program. No matter the department a faculty member may be in, we posit that successful faculty adoption of technology requires five essential elements: 1) professional development, 2) time, 3) resources (including technical support personnel), 4) teaching experience, and 5) reflection.

Rich content that can engage and empower students in the learning process should be the result of authentic technology integration. While a deep understanding of the content by the instructor is a given in the higher education classroom, we suggest that some instructors may lack similar confidence where technology integration is involved. Intentional use of technology in the classroom requires five essential elements starting with intentional planning. The gathering of resources and design support personnel are foundational in this planning process. Once these resources and personnel are in place, instructors need time to build confidence with technologies that they will be using in the classroom. It is ongoing support and practice that helps to provide the confidence and comfort that is needed to leverage technology effectively. We would also pose that the effectiveness of these practices can be fully realized only through reflective thinking and feedback.

Professional Development

Regardless of an instructor's background, professional development is critical in technology implementation. For most faculty members, the words "professional development" translate to "meaningless meeting" or "waste of time." In order for professional development to be effective, it needs to be meaningful in a variety of ways. Systemic learning in the framework of curriculum delivery modification should be contextualized. So many times the first introduction to a technology focuses on the "bells and whistles" rather than a real world example of implementation. Regardless of the modality of a professor's delivery, there needs to be "scaffolding" opportunities for each to provide an avenue to implementation in the classroom. Here is an example from a faculty member at Florida A&M University [Full faculty names are provided at the end of this chapter. Last names are provided with specific quotations in the text.]:

Faculty were trained through a professional development lecture via interactive video from a subject-matter expert and, subsequently, by our on-campus technology specialists. Our technology specialists are always available when needed and are a vital part of faculty's professional and technological development. Interactive video conferencing technology has been an excellent investment for the College. Participating in online teaching has forced me to think differently about content delivery. (Reams)

Expected outcomes not only should be demonstrated but also modeled for instructors. This initial overview of the possibilities and "how to's" of operation necessitate follow-up and individualized experiences tailored to each instructor's delivery. In some instances, this support can be provided in informal meetings between classes, while in other cases direct observation and assistance is provided to enrich the learning process.

> *We were provided outstanding training by our technology specialist at the remote campus prior to the start of fall classes. The specialist sat in on all classes the first semester and saved the day when cameras needed adjusting or when we simply missed the cue to extend the recording so that we could include students at the remote campus in the after class Q&A sessions.* (Reams)

While external expertise and specialized support personnel are good to have in the initial phases, ongoing organic cultural changes in the implementation of technology are typically driven by the faculty members themselves. This could arise as an outgrowth of a departmental meeting, in a one-to-one conversation between faculty members, through idea exchanges at conferences, or through formalized professional learning communities. The trust between faculty members and their "real-world" shared experiences are foundational for sustainability and ongoing professional development.

> *This is important as there needs to be a strong degree of competency on the instructor's part for the integration of technology within the classroom. Professional development is useful for those who will be using the technology. Faculty championing the technology are the likeliest candidates to instruct and train other faculty.* (Delacruz)

Once these conversations have begun, then faculty implementation begins to increase. The realization of what can be done is no longer conceptualized at the "trainer" or "support staff" level. Rather, it grows between courses as the instructional team begins to ask, "Can we...?" or "How would we...?" with the technologies at their disposal. These inquiry-based learning opportunities are some of the most satisfying professional development processes for the instructor. However, inevitably, the issue of "time" arises.

> *I have pursued training with technical instructors and experienced teachers who have successfully integrated interactive video into their curriculum. However, exploring possibilities takes time and energy.* (Delacruz)

Time

Purposeful use of technology in the classroom requires intentional planning. Time is one of the most valued commodities of faculty. Between, teaching, research, publishing, and the myriad of small tasks or individual hours spent working with students, faculty members struggle to find the time necessary to build confidence with technologies that they will be using in the classroom.

> *Some of the initial challenges incurred dealt with the amount of time it takes to become familiar with the technology whether through in-service training or through tutorials. As with anything new, patience and practice is a must.* (Reams)

One effective way to recover resources is to allow faculty members to leverage the same teaching technologies as a part of their learning. Too many times technologies are thrust upon instructors as an "add on" to their already complicated work schedule. When these tools can be leveraged as a conduit for their own learning, research, or as an engagement strategy with other colleagues, the impact becomes part of their daily schedule. They will then extrapolate the opportunities to leverage the given tool in their courses.

> *The key to successfully integrating the use of technologies, like Telepresence, is to afford the instructor the time and the opportunity to explore the technology. In my experience, I have relied on technical assistance and instruction. I have explored possibilities and asked questions; I have imagined scenarios and sought help to make them a reality.* (Delacruz)

Leveraging the tool to help the instructor recover time brings the realization of its implementation lifecycle. This experience of personal learning via the tool(s) gives rise to ideas on other ways the institution could authentically use the tool for other collaborative tasks. We have seen, for example, video portals used by financial aid advisors in an institution's business office to connect with students when the students have questions. Launching on-demand synchronous video calls with academic advisors or professors during virtual office hours are other ways to drive adoption and increase comfort with the technology on the part of instructors, administrators, and students. Once this adoption process begins, a technology becomes a part of the organization's culture, and no longer do faculty members feel as if they are incorporating a "one off" solution. On the contrary, there is an understanding that this is a part of who "we" are. In order for this to become a reality, however, the commitment to resources by the institution's leadership team must be in place.

Resources

The resources necessary to utilize technologies at the institution level impact the organization at a variety of levels. The previously mentioned professional development should be an outgrowth of planning and procedures adopted by the organization. At minimum, there should be consideration for technical support, implementation with other extended technologies, and financial remuneration for the faculty who are impacted.

Technical support appears at any variety of areas within an institution of higher learning. Usually technicians that assist during setup and/or when challenges arise are the front-line response teams that keep the faculty at ease while delivering content.

> *While we have the technology, it is difficult to utilize it without an expert in close proximity to assist us when an issue arises.* (Reams)

Most universities committed to an extensive technology implementation also leverage support for their faculty via instructional technologists. This technology group is typically responsible for assisting faculty members in a myriad of tasks including instructional design, content delivery, and course logistics that can arise when teaching in a technology-enabled environment.

Development of an online or blended course requires time and considerable effort. To this end, finding appropriate digital media and engaging case examples or blogs can be extremely time consuming. I am of the opinion that calculating extra effort toward an instructor's assignment of responsibility for online and blended courses should be mandatory. Student engagement in such courses requires that instructors become intimately involved with using technology and learning management systems, solving dynamic problems for students who may not be in close proximity to the main campus, and instituting remedial, online techniques for those who may not grasp important concepts. Though one might argue that these responsibilities are consistent whether courses are traditional, online, or blended, it has been my experience that online and blended courses require much more time and effort to achieve the same goal. In light of the aforementioned challenge, I must acknowledge the importance of our technology experts in the college. I would not have been able to be successful in this venture without them. (Honeywell)

While a primary technology may serve as a conduit for teaching and learning, the supporting ancillary technologies help differentiate one instructional technique from another. Instructors may be challenged in nontraditional, technology-facilitated environments to feel like they are "connecting" with students. Tools like the learning management system, collaboration tools, supplementary multi-media, individual devices, etc. can overwhelm the process if not carefully organized to be leveraged for the right task, at the right time.

Imbedded within every online lecture were video content and case examples. Most videos were obtained from YouTube to accent course outcomes. (Honeywell)

Financial incentives for technology adoption and use can be a defining factor for some programs. These programs may not necessarily provide dollars to the instructor but may provide other opportunities of value. We applaud administrations when they consider various avenues to support instructors. Course relief and extra funds toward course materials for courses taught via distance learning are two that are frequently used by universities.

Many professors at the college have become strong proponents of collaboration, helped along by a unique College of Education program that offers professors courseload relief so that they can invest time in developing new course pedagogies. The College of Education is dedicated to attracting future teachers who believe that the classroom is only one facet of the learning experience and who are committed to finding new ways to optimize learning and maximize student engagement. Our culture rewards faculty innovation in the classroom. (Edick)

Teaching Experience

At the end of the day, the best-intentioned technology procurements become instantly obsolete if there is no "reason" to leverage them in course delivery. As previously mentioned the easiest way to talk about what can be done is to have faculty experience the process as learners. Faculty must be allowed to venture down a previously unavailable opportunity to promote growth. The comments below are an outgrowth of systemic professional development with the appropriate resource mechanisms to maximize a particular technology tool suite. This process is allowing instructors to engage in a different way with their students and peers.

Courses can and should be enhanced via real-world experiences and expertise. This authentic, application-based approach to learning can be facilitated by a variety of technologies infused into the daily process of course delivery.

> *Interactive video enables ambitions in the scope of the project you set your students. We are no longer limited by geography. An advertising class in San Jose can easily work on a brief set by an ad agency in London, New York, or Sydney. We benefit from added networking opportunities.* (Delacruz)

This expertise can move beyond a specialist in the field to building relationships between future colleagues regardless of their geography. Real-time, transparent community building technologies are the reality of the business world. These experiences prepare tomorrow's workforce for that reality while helping them acknowledge their preparation (or lack thereof) to compete.

> *Another way that interactive video enhanced the student experience was through a partnership that has continued to grow. As with the previous case study this example was born from prior experience where a collaborative exercise between students at two different institutions relied on the physical space offered by an*

advertising agency. This need for a physical space becomes problematic when one college is situated in the California and the other in New York. Interactive video has proven an invaluable connector and has allowed relationships between institutions to blossom. In this case students from the advertising program at San Jose State worked in collaboration with advertising students from Syracuse University. They were teamed, introduced, and briefed via interactive video. The live experience may have been digital, but it was as effective as the previous real experiences. Student teams had to work online—some chose Skype, some Facebook, some email. They shared and edited work digitally and then submitted their creative solutions electronically. The debrief and feedback occurred live via interactive video.

My class in San Jose participated in a collaborative project with a similar class in New York, Vienna and Berlin. These two examples have always been possible, but they require travel and expense. Interactive video helps us bring other experts into the classroom we may not have been able to bring in before. It adds value to our students' learning experience and enhances the knowledge they develop. Interactive video effectively helps us to imagine endless possibilities that can only help to push curricula into new and exciting directions. There are learning opportunities that arise because of the development of new digital technologies. Spending time learning, as an instructor, only serves to enhance the delivery of the teaching experience and, thus, enhances the students' learning experience too.
(Delacruz)

The experience of teaching continues to morph as a variety of technologies and possibilities emerge. At first, the traditional classroom model was reshaped via innovations that influenced the way direct large-group instruction was delivered. However, the modality of delivery stayed the same.

Identifying student needs and finding out how to make the technology work for you can only be achieved by experience. (Delacruz)

Next, the opportunity brought forth as a result of the individual device surfaced. If every student has their own tool, can that tool become a conduit for individual contribution and interaction with the instructor as well as with other students? Students can now prepare individually on their devices by gleaning content traditionally reserved for onsite lecture and be prepared to discuss and make application when they arrive. Collaborative technologies are helping transform conventional teaching routines and allowing teachers to spend more time interacting with students, resulting in less reliance on lecturing. Many courses in the programs are hybrids that combine the flexibility of an online program with the face-to-face experience of a traditional physical classroom.

The time constraints are further removed when direct course delivery opportunities are delivered at a time that is convenient for both instructor and student. Using the right tool, for the right task at the right time respects both teacher's and learner's most valuable commodity, time.

University of Nebraska Omaha College of Education offers a unique online master's degree program in special education with a "behavior disorder" concentration. The college now offers the option of an online distance-learning program that uses a variety of interactive videoconferencing and other collaborative technologies to make it easy for non-local students to remotely attend classes. Several of the program's classes are conducted via live online lectures, using WebEx conferencing and desktop sharing. Additional course content is disseminated through weekly learning modules in which students participate in asynchronous group discussions using blogs, Wikis, and posts in Blackboard, the college's learning management system. Such discussions are monitored and facilitated by professors, who are also available during flexible "virtual" office hours via one-on-one chats in Cisco's Jabber or Skype.

"Scaffolding" or blending these technologies can provide further opportunities to reach students with a variety of learner styles and needs. This experience allows for instructors to organically grow their personal styles into a satisfying technology-enhanced experience for both themselves and their learners.

Though I have taught previously within a blended online course, my challenge was to innovatively incorporate Crestview students into my lecture such that they felt included and engaged. To accomplish this feat, I intently asked questions of the Tallahassee and Crestview groups every 10-15 minutes during lecture. Engaging and calculated questions afforded me the opportunity to discern whether students truly grasped important concepts or whether I needed to remediate such concepts using interactive video or our learning management system.
(Honeywell)

When these tools are repurposed outside traditional course delivery, their impact can be transformational for the institution on the whole. At that point, the culture of the organization shifts. The technology is no longer something we discuss; it becomes a transparent conduit for communication.

> *The interactive video technology is used to bridge the gap from the distant campus to the main campus on a daily basis. One of the ways the services are utilized is for a tutoring program entitled "Rx Care," which is an academic success program that provides encouragement and support designed to enhance student academic achievement. This program provides services that include but are not limited to peer tutoring, supplemental instruction, success coaching, improvement of study habits, stress/time management, and note taking strategies.* (Reams)

However, one of the cultural concerns is the protection of ideas and research. As is the case with any innovation, technological or otherwise, the people doing the innovating (in this case the faculty) need to have full assurance that their intellectual property remains their own. These concerns become more real with the propagation of a variety of tools.

> *I think that none of our lectures should be pirated, and there should be a warning that this is the property of FAMU and Professor XYZ and should not be distributed without written consent from Professor XYZ.* (Reams)

> *All content should be protected by intellectual property laws. Such laws must be a requisite part of online instruction.* (Honeywell)

Policy surrounding these issues needs to be addressed proactively rather than reactively. Just as proper resources were allocated as support mechanisms to the tools themselves, so too should appropriate resources be allocated to the protection of the persons leveraging those tools. However, all possible issues may not be foreseeable prior to embarking on the implementation journey. That is why reflection and refinement are necessary to continue the evolution.

Reflection

The growth process for instructors is sustained through feedback via course evaluations, instructor reflection, and peer review. These are critical components for the effectiveness of technology adoption beyond initial training or workshops.

In the higher education realm, student course satisfaction contributes to course and degree completion. Formal and informal feedback throughout the process helps faculty gauge successful (or unsuccessful) technology implementation. Student feedback from courses using a web-based conferencing technology for synchronous office hours and synchronous class sessions stated that the ability to receive immediate feedback from instructors and classmates allowed for a greater understanding of the material. Additionally, the instructors that use web-based conferencing technology describe the level of engagement in their online courses as more positive and said it allows them to assess the student's level of understanding far better than just asynchronous communication within the discussion forums of the learning management system.

Faculty member feedback to and through the support mechanisms outlined above also help shape the continued evolution of technology implementation on campus. These reflections should be a part of ongoing dialogue and exchange between technical support, instructional support and administrative branches of the institution. Without open lines of communication, faculty members can begin to feel isolated and frustrated with the process of technology implementation.

> *As a faculty member working away from the main campus, it can sometimes be easy to feel as if one is not part of the team; however, with the Telepresence technology, opportunities that at first seemed impossible are now beginning to become the wave of the future.* (Reams)

These reflections also help shape refinements that can further enhance future iterations of a course. Many of these faculty "ah-ha" moments grow directly from the experience of leveraging the tool in direct instruction.

> *I foresee the possibility of switching online pedagogy from conventional lectures to a flipped classroom. Flipped classrooms force students to assume responsibility for viewing recorded lectures and reading required content prior to class. As such, in an effort to clarify misunderstood concepts, the Telepresence classroom would only be employed to galvanize instructor- and student-led group discussions and for students to actively participate in case examples. Moreover, flipped classrooms encourage students to realize the importance of individualized and life-long learning and how to approach mastery of these skills.* (Honeywell)

Interactive video technology has enabled me to do much more than I could do before I integrated it into my curriculum. The opportunities it affords the instructor and the student are invaluable. (Delacruz)

I have noticed a higher level of my students' depth of understanding. This is due to the students' ability to play back the video whenever and wherever they want. (Surface)

A faculty member's willingness to share such valuable insights has the potential to effect entire academic departments and, quite possibly, the entire institution.

Collaboration adoption by students and faculty are key to the College of Education administration reaching its goals of introducing new programs and education models, recruiting high-quality faculty, attracting non-local students, and enhancing and expanding the college's brand reputation as a regional leader in many programs. Collaboration solutions facilitate innovation and student-centered learning. The bottom line is that collaboration technologies can open the door to new opportunities and generate enthusiasm for learning. It is especially exciting to continue to raise the quality of distance learning with the use of technology. (Edick)

Conclusion

From our work with educational institutions, we conclude that the acquisition and implementation of technology for technology's sake in teaching and learning environments is pointless for the institution. Rather, identifying a challenge or "flashpoint" provides focus and direction to procurement and the supporting processes that need to be in place to bring the vision to fruition. These supporting processes should be at minimum professional development, time considerations, resources to support the process, measurable impact on teaching and learning experiences, and opportunity for reflection by those impacted by the technology. With these considerations we believe that technology can become "teachnology."

RESOURCES

Rogers, E. (1995). *Diffusion of innovations.* (4th ed.). New York: Simon & Schuster.

Stubbs, W. (2009). "Innovators to Laggards: How to Work With All Faculty Members." Retrieved from: http://www.uwex.edu/disted/conference/Resource_library/proceedings/09_20196.pdf

Faculty that have contributed their insight and content for this chapter:

Adcock, Phyllis, College of Education, University Nebraska Omaha

Delacruz, John, Advertising, San Jose State University

Edick, Nancy, Dean, College of Education, University Nebraska Omaha

Honeywell, Marlon S., Professor, College of Pharmacy and Pharmaceutical Sciences, Florida A&M University

Leader Janssen, Elizabeth, College of Education, University Nebraska Omaha

Reams, R. Renee, College of Pharmacy and Pharmaceutical Sciences, Florida A&M University

Surface, Jeanne, College of Education, University of Nebraska Omaha

---

DR. LANCE FORD, is an Education Advocate on the Cisco Education Team. Lance's primary job responsibility is to work with educators who are leveraging both synchronous and asynchronous tools to engage their learners. These educators want the learning experience to be participatory and authentic while the role of the technology remains simply that of conduit. Prior to working in this role, Dr. Ford was a public school teacher for 15 years and worked adjunct for the University of Maine system for a couple of years. In addition to working with faculty, Lance is also currently team-teaching a course in humanities. He's been recognized as an Apple Distinguished Educator, Wal-Mart Regional Teacher of the Year, and Oklahoma's Outstanding Director of Technology. Lance's goal in working with educators is to provide a hands-on, real-world engagement that fosters faculty extrapolation of the possibilities into their own curricular areas.

MARY SCHLEGELMILCH is an Education Advocate on the Cisco Education Team. Mary is dedicated to education and the integration of technology that will empower and engage teaching and learning environments. Mary connects with educators globally to assist educational institutions as they incorporate collaborative solutions via video from the Cisco Collaboration Rooms at the University of Nebraska Omaha. Prior to her current role at Cisco, Mary has worked with elementary and secondary students in both rural and urban schools as an early childhood educator and a middle school science teacher. Her experience as a district curriculum facilitator and as the eLearning Supervisor in charge of online, blended, and distance education in a large metropolitan school district allowed her to integrate synchronous and asynchronous tools into learning environments.

Chapter 5

IT Leadership

Chapter 5

IT Leadership

"We tend to overestimate the effect of a technology in the short run and underestimate the effect in the long run."
—Roy Amara[1]

By Tracy Futhey

Successful Information Technology (IT) leadership actually is fairly straightforward, and at its most basic simply is a matter of having a Chief Information Officer (CIO) or other similar leader who:

- Works closely with academic leadership to stay abreast of the local campus needs and anticipate IT-related implications for higher education;
- Tracks technology trends and identifies ways in which IT can support the local community and advance the goals and strategies of the university;
- Locates willing and able partners who will experiment with new technologies, new applications of existing technologies, and new uses and combinations of data; and
- Deploys and supports those technologies with the right balance of speed-to-market, functionality or feature set, stability and security.

---

[1] Roy Amara (1925-2007) was a researcher, scientist, and past president of the Institute for the Future. Born in Boston in 1925, he has also worked at Stanford Research Institute. Source: Wikipedia.

As straightforward as that might be on the surface, actually delivering on it successfully and consistently can be complicated.

Knowledge of the Campus and Higher Education

IT leadership needs to engage with deans and academic leaders to identify and reinforce ways in which technology can help meet *their* goals. All too often IT is considered a back office function or is relegated in the minds of leaders as "just infrastructure" that can be either taken for granted or deferred for later consideration in a project. It is not. Nor is it the case that "IT management should, frankly, become boring" as Nicholas Carr wrote in 2003[2]. IT remains one of the most powerful and essential components of delivering any new service or program today, and without fully considering and accounting for its impact early in a project, we risk gaffes strategically—missed opportunities or ill-advised approaches—or financially through wasted resources.

The placement of the CIO role (or other IT leadership) and the organization structure on an individual campus may make this task easier or harder. Surveys[3] over the years of CIOs in higher education indicate that CIO reporting is typically to the President/Chancellor, Provost or EVP/CFO. In those cases where the CIO reports to the President and is a part of the

---

[2] *IT Doesn't Matter,* Harvard Business Review, Nicholas G. Carr, May 2003.

[3] EDUCAUSE's 2011, *The Higher Education CIO* Research Report based from its annual Core Data Survey reported that approximately 34% of CIO reporting to the highest-ranking administrative or business officer, 30% reporting to the president or chancellor, and 26% reporting to the highest-ranking academic officer. They further noted that reporting structures had not changed appreciably from 2003-2011.

President's Cabinet, the positioning of the role reinforces its strategic importance, and the CIO has natural visibility. Here the objective of visibility goes beyond the CIO being present in the minds of the cabinet, institutional leaders, and the board of trustees or regents; it is the importance of the CIO having visibility and insight *into* the plans and directions of the university as they are being developed. Without knowledge of strategic initiatives at the earliest stage possible, it will be difficult for the CIO to anticipate the ways in which the evolution of the campus needs and higher education generally can be most fully enabled and supported through the appropriate use of IT.

While Presidential reporting and Cabinet participation for the CIO may make it easier for IT to be a part of strategic conversations, it is by no means necessary to achieving effective IT leadership. A CIO reporting to the chief academic or administrative officer can be just as effective but needs engagement and visibility into strategic decision-making to ensure IT remains aligned with the institution's goals and evolving programs. In a large and decentralized research university this often involves a great deal of community building and establishment of goodwill, especially if there are historical tendencies to siloed operations (the "every tub on its own bottom" model) or distrust of central IT at the school or departmental level. Establishing trust and goodwill is a necessary precondition for the CIO who is faced with improving visibility in a structure where the CIO reports deeper in the organization.

Not only is the IT leader's ability to gain appropriate visibility into decision making influenced by structure and reporting lines, it is also inextricably linked to the university's culture for centralized or decentralized decision making. A culture of decentralized decision making and action will require much greater community and trust building in order for IT to be recognized as relevant to the discussion when strategic issues are at play: If local IT leaders and individual faculty don't trust central IT to deliver great services and support the routine technologies in their lives—email, network access, classroom technology support—they are unlikely to be very supportive of the CIO interjecting opinions regarding how they might use IT more fully to enable their strategic, emerging programs.

Certain deans and academic leaders may be very technologically savvy and some may be quick to promote—or stave off—the IT in advancing new programs or priorities. Relying on any single viewpoint in making those decisions, be it the CIO's or another leader's, is likely to be suboptimal for the institution. As with all decisions, they are best arrived at through informed debate and the give-and-take that emerges from the discussion of those with different perspectives and domain expertise. The CIO either needs to be involved in those discussions by virtue of organization structure and positioning or needs to use personal and organizational credibility and influence to make a way into those discussions. In this way community building will lead to trust building, which will lead to the establishment of goodwill, which will be an essential element of the CIO's success.

IT as an Enabling Force in Education

We are in a world that is changing radically as a direct result of IT. The level of ubiquity and access to information afforded by low-cost mobile devices has changed the way we live, work and play. The fact that handheld devices are more powerful and capable than computers of just a decade ago, and will continue to become exponentially more powerful over time, was first is observed in 1965 by Moore's Law.[4]

In 2004—three years before the introduction of the iPhone— Duke launched its iPod project to explore the relevance of mobile devices to a Duke education. There was a good deal of national attention around the project, much of it heralding Duke for its forward-looking perspective, but some of it criticizing Duke for what it claimed was a misguided program supporting devices that were "just" music players. Duke pursued the project because we saw the potential that even those early and limited *digital media players* would evolve into powerful mobile technologies. And in embracing even the imperfect and incomplete technology available at that early stage, Duke was able to stimulate a dialog on campus about the ways in which IT might enhance the delivery of educational content to a future student learner using technology that was intuitive to use and where access was seamless and ubiquitous. That dialog has continued and led to many other projects and innovations: from lecture capture technology and flipped or hybrid class approaches, to digital innovation programs that involve students in technology experimentation and development. None of these likely would have been launched or would have evolved as quickly as they did, were it not for that first, bold experiment.

Clearly today the impact and ubiquity of mobile devices is far and wide and embraces not only how we play (music and otherwise), but also how we learn and work. Already our campus networks connect as many or more mobile devices than

---

[4] See https://en.wikipedia.org/wiki/Moore%27s_law

laptops, desktops and servers, and very soon their popularity will overtake that of "computers" in the style of desktops or laptops. For most of us we are always connected through one device or another. So while we may not always be *on it,* "it" is always or nearly always *on us.*

In less than 10 years we have moved from a debate about whether mobile devices even had a place as productivity tools to a time when we're never without them and rely on them constantly for checking email, assignments, calendars, maps, directions, and virtually everything else. That pervading character of IT in our lives **will never slow down**. In fact, so long as Moore's Law persists and the rate at which technology changes remains exponential, the new capabilities afforded by that technology will lead to an ever more embedded role of IT in all aspects of our lives. And because the technology will not only be ever more powerful but also more affordable, the pace of change it enables will be dizzying. This will result in new technologies coming to market more affordably and with new relevance and applicability to higher education. And each of these will continue to improve exponentially over time.

Consider the range of technologies relevant to higher education as illustrated along the Gartner's 2014 Hype Cycle for Education[5] (see next page):

Without regard to the placement of specific technologies on this curve at a given time, the important takeaway is the phasing of technology evolution, from the "Peak of Inflated Expectations" when technology is gaining exposure and our

---

[5] *Hype Cycle for Education, 2014,* Gartner Research Note, 23 July 2014, G00263196, Jan-Martin Lowendahl

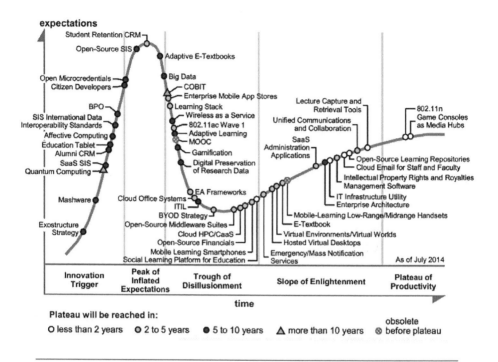

expectations run ahead of the practical reality of its impact, to the "Trough of Disillusionment" as the technology penetrates the market and the technology's limitations and problems invariability cause us to underestimate technology's long-run impact.

As for the argument from those who claim IT will have a limited impact on higher education, that argument is fundamentally flawed. While it is true that higher education has persisted in largely the same form it has taken for centuries, in this era of technological change it is irrational to accept and embrace technology's role in fundamentally changing nearly every aspect of our personal lives on a daily basis, without also recognizing the inevitability that it will change higher education just as profoundly. That is not to say that technology will bring an end to the residential campus experience, but it is certainly the case that the thoughtful application of IT will profoundly change the way education occurs, even within the presumed sanctity of a residential campus. Future students who elect to attend residential-based campuses will utilize IT as a part of their learning process in ways that are fundamentally different than how mainstream education is delivered today, including more learner-centered and participatory environments that are enabled and mediated by technology, and where the faculty role begins to shift from the front of the room to the "guide by the side" orientation.[6]

The challenge for IT leadership in this context is twofold: to not only track the wide range of relevant technologies over their lifecycle, but also to evaluate where the individual technologies can advance campus programs and priorities or can contribute to strategic goals. Unlike the IT environment in the 1980s when it was possible for one or two universities whose names were synonymous with technology to influence the dialog nationally around IT innovation[7], today we see a democratization of opportunity around IT innovation with each point in the graphic above—and many technologies not even represented there—providing an opportunity for IT leadership through the thoughtful analysis and selection of strategic areas of deployment of IT or new use cases or applications of technology. Beyond technology's impact in the way education is delivered, IT is now mediating changes in the very nature of the workforce by democratizing access to information

---

[6] https://chronicle.com/article/Professors-Place-in-the/149975/?cid=at&utm_source=at&utm_medium=en

[7] Consider Project Athena a joint project from 1983-1991 among MIT, Digital Equipment Corporation and IBM to produce a campus-wide distributed computing environment for educational use. (Source: Wikipedia)

and resources. What Uber has demonstrated is not just the power of an app for finding transportation; it demonstrates the power of putting consumers—of any given product—in direct touch with potential suppliers in a way that vastly simplifies how they consume that product. Extensions of that model into other aspects of workforce development (TaskRabbit, for example) could have significant implication for how universities receive and provide goods and services.

The iPod example at Duke referenced earlier is quite modest, especially in comparison to programs like MIT's Project Athena; but it does reinforce the importance of IT leadership continuously scanning the technology domain for trends and ways in which IT might be applied on a given campus—in big or small ways—at a particular moment. Sometimes that may be an opportunistic project aimed at raising exposure or changing the dialog on the campus. At other times it may be a fundamental change in how systems must be more directly interconnected so as to share data seamlessly, or a new system altogether that has a unique ability to serve an emerging need. Whatever the use, IT is the enabler for all that we do, and it can be applied in different ways and at different times to meet the particular needs of a campus.

There will also be occasions where the careful tracking and planning of technology applications will allow the CIO to identify opportunities for the campus to skip or leapfrog technologies, such as those campuses that were able to defer their legacy administrative (or ERP, Enterprise Resource Planning) systems long enough to move directly to cloud-based solutions, foregoing the 10-15 year interim transition to on-premises ERP architectures. Another example of technology skipping might be supporting WiFi exclusively (rather than wired networks) in a new building, or moving from 802.11g to 802.11ac, skipping a generation of WiFi. Of course, such decisions depend on the intensity of the IT uses by relevant constituents and the willingness of those individuals to be early test cases into the latest, not-yet-mainstream technologies that enable new capabilities.

Such technology skipping approaches could also facilitate new, advanced exploration, such as the capabilities available through mobile and ubiquitous high-speed access to technology within the campus. Throughout, the IT leader needs to set appropriate expectations and take care in prompting even part of the campus toward the leading edge, without inadvertently taking it over the bleeding edge.

The Importance and Selection of Partnerships

Perhaps most important to being able to exploit the power of IT on a campus is the IT leader's ability to identify and attract strong partners willing to experiment with new technologies, or to explore new applications of existing technologies. Disruptive change is already occurring related to pedagogy and the role technology can play in supporting and enhancing learning. Flipped or hybrid (partially online, partially in-person) teaching methods are bringing a greater level of flexibility to the student learning environment. There has been much debate about whether this is a good thing or a bad thing for higher education, but irrespective of one's individual opinion, the point is that it is a thing, and it is going to continue to have an impact. Claims that universities should ignore these new technologies or approaches are not unlike the arguments a decade ago that campus IT leaders should turn off WiFi in classrooms so that students would pay closer attention to the lecture. Not only do substitute technologies exist (e.g., cellular in the WiFi example), but there are also substitute distractions even if the computer or smartphone is powered off (including old-fashioned technologies like a print version of the student newspaper). So rather than deciding that some technologies are fit for exploration and others should be ignored, the CIO needs to be identifying appropriate and willing partners to pursue a range of different projects. This is more difficult than it sounds, since the opportunity has to be so promising that the partner will pursue it enthusiastically rather than grudgingly. When it comes to partners for the IT organization, a half-hearted or grudging partner is worse than no partner at all.

Faculty as Academic Partners—Teaching Innovation and Enabling Pedagogy Change. Willing faculty need to be sought out to explore and trial new technology-enabled pedagogical approaches. Not all of these trials will succeed and so there needs to be a strong commitment of the institutional leadership to pursue multiple experiments in various domains, and to support the adaptation of approaches in a more nimble way than is often characteristic of higher education. In today's rapidly changing technology environment, characterized by exponential improvements in technology, often it is not practical to spend years or even many months studying an emerging academic technology opportunity before making a decision about how to pursue it. And even if a decision is made with relative acuity, the pace of technology change today often means we can't use an historic approach to project planning, where multiple stakeholder groups are convened to establish requirements after which a Request for Proposals is issued and reviewed before the project is formally launched. Rather, multiple projects and partners, pursuing multiple approaches or pilot projects, will be a much more effective strategy. By partnering with faculty and enabling multiple, smaller experiments, the outcomes will not only be much faster, but also will reflect the reality that no single solution or approach is likely to work for all situations. And as a secondary consequence, this approach to partnering will likely result in faculty champions who can carry the message with a higher level of credibility to their colleagues. Opportunities for IT leadership in this domain include exploration around interactive and online learning modules, problem-based and project-based pedagogical approaches, adaptive and interactive e-textbooks, micro-credentialing, reusable repositories of video course materials (i.e., "snippits"), and others.

Student Innovators and Citizen Developers. Among the greatest untapped assets for IT organizations on campuses are the individual students and faculty and their personal curiosity and capability in devising new applications of IT. The mobile app store model combined with cloud-based systems and capabilities has ushered in a new era of "citizen developers" who can easily take an idea for a product from conception to implementation in a matter of weeks or months. Because the products they develop then have mass-market access via mobile app stores, central IT or the CIO in particular is no longer able to lead the campus down a specific, unified, "supported" path of IT infrastructure. Rather, every individual has become empowered—whether central IT or the institutional leadership likes it or not—to define their own environment and download, **or build themselves,** the applications that enable the features they seek. For this reason, partnering or at least enabling the individual citizen developers on a campus will be particularly important in the coming years. In terms of strategies, this will mean much more than the sort of contests or competition emerging today that engage students and challenge them to develop apps.[8,9] Here, consider the importance of formal programs to make institutional data available and easy to use, to assist with "hardening" proof-of-concept student apps, to provide design and "user experience" expertise, and to provide distribution and advertising channels for technologies built by our citizen developers, especially when they improve the IT environment and systems of the university.

Business Unit Leaders as Administrative Partners. Administrators within central business units of the university have long been partners to the CIO, especially in the era of retiring legacy business systems in favor of modern, enterprise-scale ERP systems supporting those business units. Looking forward, the so-called drive toward *big data* and data analytics has the potential to fundamentally change several aspects of existing campus business operations and usher in new capabilities within the administration of higher education that arise from data aggregation and analytics at a scale not previously enabled on campuses. Although significant amounts of rich data exist on our campuses today, because those data tend to be siloed we have not been successful in exploiting the potential that comes from combining and correlating the data and enabling its use in real time. In this regard, the CIO has natural partners in the various administrative and business owners of the institutions—the Registrar, leaders for student affairs, curricular planning, student advising, and many others.

Faculty and Students Perspectives in Partnerships. It is essential that a range of perspectives be brought to the table as the CIO seeks to chart the course for the campus IT

---

8 http://cic.gatech.edu/
9 http://today.duke.edu/2013/02/colab

environment. Faculty experts from a wide range of domains can be sought out: engineering and computer science faculty with interest in Software Defined Networking, security, wireless and mobility; public policy faculty with expertise in big data, net neutrality and Internet policy; economics and business faculty who focus on cloud services, economics of technical change, pricing and resource management in networked systems; sociology faculty regarding the effects of social networks, and many others. The opportunity here is to tap the university's internal resource base rather than presuming that such expertise should be sought from consultant outside the institution. Beyond their domain expertise, faculty can be ideal partners in the university's quest to enable inter-institutional research and collaboration.

Likewise, students have become increasingly important as collaborators for the forward-looking university and IT organization. Beyond their role as 'citizen developers', they bring a necessary perspective as *digital natives* who have grown up living and breathing technology in ways that those of us above the age of 25 have not. Tapping in to their perspectives surfaces important expectations for how the campus should use IT and how students will experience it. This will be essential for the CIO to deliver an IT environment that remains relevant and useful to the evolving needs of future students.

Industry Partnerships. Finally, industry partners can be a key element of success for IT leadership. Targeting and engaging industry partners early in a technology's lifecycle can often bring financial incentives if the industry collaborator recognizes the value of breaking into a new market with a trusted university partner. Not only does this approach allow the university early access to emerging technologies, and at a lower cost than later adopters; benefits can accrue to the university user base and IT organization through that early exploration of technologies and the knowledge gained from early experimentation can provide important lessons for future deployments as the technologies move up the deployment and maturity curve. It can also provide useful leverage with vendors who will tend to favor engagement with universities that have a strong grasp of the technology and what it can enable.

Data's Unique Role Enabling Partnerships. Although higher education does not necessarily have a high time utility for data—unlike the financial industry or supply-chain management within manufacturing where real-time decision making and transaction processing can mean revenue gains or losses of millions of dollars in minutes—there are aspects of higher education that can benefit from more immediate data analytics availability. In fact, each of the partnership opportunities described above relates in one way or another to access, correlation, and analysis of data.

Consider citizen developers and faculty researchers. The more complex, but also much more powerful, change that needs to occur to empower and support them is the loosening of the reigns on institutional data such that student and faculty development can be enabled. Data on campuses often is siloed, with the cognizant business administrator over the function being the *data owner* or *data steward* and the person with near autonomous decision-making over whether or how the data from those systems can be accessed or used by others. This has contributed over time to the siloed nature of the data, but also limits into the future the institution's ability to fully leverage the citizen developer model. Related, faculty researchers may benefit a great deal from access to institutional data, such as sharing anonymized network traffic data with computer science researchers. The CIO has an essential role in advocating for making data available for appropriate and authorized uses, while simultaneously putting into place reasonable protections and data usage agreements.

Not only can appropriate access to data enable citizen developers, but it can also support new and important institutional uses of data with and across business units. One such area is tracking student engagement (class attendance, use of the learning management system, co-curricular activities and even social media interactions, just to name a few) as a way to identify trends or make interventions that may lead to improved retention and academic progression. This has become an interesting opportunity, especially within publics where funding may be tied to retention or graduation rates.

Data analysis at a massive scale also holds promise for its potential to contribute improvement within the realm of teaching and learning. There is much that still needs to be learned through the tracking and correlation of how students are using materials from flipped classes, interactive textbooks, online tutorials and assessments, and how the use of those materials related to prior and future success of the student in attainment of learning outcomes. Even as Massive Open Online Courses (MOOCs) evolve rapidly from the "Peak of Inflated Expectations" (during their early introduction in 2012-13) to the "Tough of Disillusionment" (in 2014)[10,11], there is a scale of data analytics enabled through those massive cours-

---

[10] *MOOCs: Inflated Expectations, Early Disappointments,* Wall Street Journal's CIO Journal, December 27, 2013, http://blogs.wsj.com/cio/2013/12/27/moocs-inflated-expectations-early-disappointments/

[11] *Data Mining Exposes Embarrassing Problems for Massive Open Online Courses,* MIT Technology Review, December 18, 2013, http://www.technologyreview.com/view/522816/data-mining-exposes-embarrassing-problems-for-massive-open-online-courses/

es that can never be matched on an individual campus. Without data at such a massive scale, it is extremely difficult or impossible to identify statistical significance in data trends regarding how students learn and the corollary of how effective specific teaching methods may be (or even the simple case of faculty receiving feedback in the form of data analytics showing which of their course recordings are most often viewed and for how long). Carnegie Mellon's Open Learning Initiative (which recently moved to Stanford)[12] is a powerful demonstration of the potential of applying cognitive science techniques to design *predictive* or *personalized learning,* wherein it is possible to anticipate the different paths that will best serve different students based on individual learning styles and studying data at a massive scale. Underestimating the power of these approaches is especially easy to do when we find ourselves the "Trough of Disillusionment" and we risk falling into the trap Amara warned of "underestimate[ing] the effect [of technology] in the long run."

Balancing IT Leadership with Support, Stability and Security

Perhaps the most essential element of successful IT leadership relates to balance. As mentioned earlier, unless basic services are routinely delivered, faculty and university leaders will have little interest in collaborating with the IT organization in strategic endeavors. This means it is crucial to find an appropriate equilibrium between the introduction of new and innovative technologies—with all of the inherent opportunities but also the lack of stability that can come along—and the

---

[12] Open Learning Pioneer Heads West, Inside Higher Ed, May 28, 2013, https://www.insidehighered.com/news/2013/05/28/candace-thille-moves-stanford

delivery of rock-solid support and stability for the institutions tried and true technologies.

The challenge in getting this balance right is for the IT organization to recognize where it needs to be somewhat contradictory in approach and service levels: being at times a basic utility and delivering routine, highly reliable services and at other times being a nimble startup trialing new services with a "best effort" approach. For example, the IT organization needs to provide traditional printing services for students that are production quality, easy to use, and always operational, while also introducing innovative and advanced services such as 3-D printing that are emerging and experimental, delivered with minimal expectation of 24/7 availability or formal support via the Help Desk operation.

Innovation in this regard is not only bringing an idea forward, it is also about the speed of introduction, the agility with which we change or "pivot" from one solution or approach to another. Innovation also requires a willingness to accept "good enough" in the near term based on an expectation that incremental improvement over time will occur, and a recognition that there is a place in early innovation releases for actively using the experience and input of the user community as a sort of living laboratory for real-time experiments to improve the product's functionality. Let's not forget Google's Gmail was a beta release product—not yet acknowledged as a traditional, production service—for more than five years and while it served tens of millions of users![13,14]

---

[13] http://googleblog.blogspot.com/2009/07/google-apps-is-out-of-beta-yes-really.html

[14] Gmail Nudges Past AOL Email In The U.S. To Take No. 3 Spot, Tech Crunch, Aug 14, 2009, http://techcrunch.com/2009/08/14/gmail-nudges-past-aol-email-in-the-us-to-take-no-3-spot/

Google is well known for its A/B tests where different segments of its user base have different interfaces that allow the developers to select the optimal user experience. This is the epitome of experimentation with a defined user base, but at massive scale. In a similar regard, the university community is a powerful (and also a somewhat captive) resource that can be effectively tapped for feedback on services so as to enable incremental, ongoing service improvement. Much of this can occur without formal institutional review boards so long as the aim is service improvemen; the data accessed are anonymous, and use is in keeping within the bounds of FERPA and other regulatory requirements. Privacy is especially important as data aggregation and correlation—even for uses that are aimed at improving IT services such as reducing unwanted emails (spam)—could unintentionally expose personal information.

Regardless of where a service is along the innovation to production spectrum, security and minimizing risk remain necessary considerations. Each day the advancing threat landscape of the Internet puts our campus at risk. Balance is especially important here as it is far too easy to believe that all IT security risks must be mitigated to the fullest extent, even if doing so results in an IT environment that is difficult to use. Here the prerequisites for successful balance will be engaged faculty governance, a well-designed IT risk communications program, campus credibility of the central IT organization (including the CIO and Chief Information Security Officer), and an executive steering or sponsoring function that includes campus leaders from the academic, administrative, legal, risk, and compliance domains.

Conclusion: The CIO's Unique Role in the Digital Revolution in Higher Education

The CIO has a unique and indispensable role in positioning the campus to meet the challenge of the digital revolution. Information Technology is a force that is not going to slow down, and as a result higher education will face opportunities and disruptive change. The irony is that IT is also the fundamental element for contending with that change, and the sooner institutions embrace the inevitable that disruptive change is ahead, the sooner they can move proactively rather than reactively.

Perspectives vary as to how quickly and through what means that inevitable change will occur. One must consider which are the most fruitful and can be turned into immediate opportunities to transform certain aspects of higher education. Considerations include, operating efficiencies achieved through automation of administrative processes, data analytics, along with enhancements to teaching approaches and student-centered or adaptive learning opportunities. At the same time one must navigate new services and approaches to support faculty research and collaboration through extending our reach and "brands" globally. Each of these is already occurring on campuses and likely to accelerate in the future, although with varying speed and penetration at the individual campus level.

The CIO can do a great deal to influence the discussion on campus, and based on the particular structure and placement of the IT organization, may need to vary the approach and path for ensuring participation in strategic conversations. But the CIO cannot effectively position the campus for this future without the help of campus leaders and faculty who will support *and embrace* the inevitable disruptions that are ahead of us all. Strong institution leadership is needed to ensure the emerging vision in how IT will be employed aligns with institutional goals and takes into account strong input from faculty to ensure the right balance of functionality and risk, as well as with engaged student input to surface approaches and perspectives of the new digital natives.

Amara's observation at the start of this chapter is also a relevant closing reminder in preparing for the future: we must avoid falling into either trap of overestimating the short-term impact or underestimating the long-term impact. In doing the former we risk wasting resources by over-committing to specific approaches when the industry is still evolving and immature. But the other trap is even more problematic since by underestimating the long term impact we may fail to commit soon enough to gain the full benefit from technology's potential over time.

In short, the successful CIO needs not to just "wait and see" but to be able to identify and predict technology change, and enable and support basic and enhanced campus IT needs. Partners can help, especially those who embrace Socrates's observation that:

> *"The secret of change is to focus all of your energy, not on fighting the old, but on building the new."*

|||||||||||||||||||||||||||||||||||||||||||||||||||||||||||||||||||||||||||||||||||||||||||||||||||||||||||||||||||||||||||||||||||||||||||||||||||||||||||||

TRACY FUTHEY, Vice President for Information Technology and Chief Information Officer

As Vice President for Information Technology and Chief Information Officer at Duke University since 2002, Tracy Futhey has presided over Duke's rise as a national leader in higher education information technology. Through programs such as the Duke Digital Initiative and its inventive use of iPods and iTunes in higher education, she has become a recognized leader in enlisting commercial technologies to create and disseminate digital course materials.

Futhey also has been the engine behind a new generation of computing capabilities across campus as well as regionally and nationally. She led the creation of the nation's first national research and education optical network, as founding chair of the National LambdaRail from 2003 to 2007. In 2008, she championed deployment of the most extensive campus-wide installation of next-generation, 802.11n wireless technologies. Futhey has also proved innovative in technology collaboration and leadership, from devising new approaches for supporting shared computing research facilities on campus to designing a new global IT infrastructure supporting Duke's international expansion.

Before Duke, Futhey spent 17 years at Carnegie Mellon, where her career spanned the range of IT, from computer consultant to CIO. As CIO, she gained a reputation as a well-rounded leader, having overseen major projects in wireless, mobile, and location-based computing.

Chapter 6

A Student Perspective

Chapter 6
A Student Perspective

By Celena Aponte

Some of the students interviewed for this chapter are experiencing the benefits of advanced technology more than others, but regardless of the starting point, there is much opportunity ahead for students, faculty, and administrators to invent and evolve. While it's unrealistic to think all students will share the experiences expressed in this chapter, I have interviewed enough of them and researched extensively key trends across the country to know this is more than a sampling of opinions and experiences—it's the future, and it's an exciting one.

> *"The mark of a learned person used to be, how much do you have in your head?"*
> —Lee Rainie, Director of Internet, Science and Technology
> Research at the Pew Research Center[1]

It's a sunny, beautiful Friday in November at San Francisco State University, and 32 undergrads are filing in for their 1 PM Creativity and Innovation class, a business management elective. They're carrying poster boards with their design research carefully mapped out, frantically doing last minute market research on their phones, and texting missing group members. The classroom is buzzing with digital and analogue energy as students prepare for their midterm presentations.

---

[1] Fast company pg. 28 Nov. 2014.

Your attention is immediately drawn to Christopher Hatzistratis. Tucked in the back corner, he's sitting in front of an Apple laptop and large Samsung android phone with no papers, no pen, nothing else but the two devices and a lot of empty desk. He's working across both machines to quickly answer questions and troubleshoot problems assigning tasks to a team scurrying around him to implement as fast as he's finding answers. Christopher's command and control is based on his ability to quickly access knowledge-using technology and then put the information directly into action. In this case, he's assigning a task to a fellow team member. These are talents of a "learned" person today.

This comes as no surprise. Almost every answer is at your fingertips, whether it's who won the basketball game, what a friend ate for breakfast, what meeting you have next, the state of the political economy in Uzbekistan.

The classroom sits firmly inside this increasingly complex and connected world. Students are inhaling more information than ever before and through their smart phones and social media networks are accustomed to shaping and creating many aspects of their lives. They want to manage their learning in the same way, using the same devices, with the same level of anytime access, gravitating to what's most relevant and entertaining to them.

An estimated 58% of U.S. adults have a smartphone, and 83% of 18- to 29-year-olds have one.[2] Whether you're Hatzistratis, a "Millennial" and "digital native"[3] who can't imagine life with-

---

[2] http://www.pewinternet.org/fact-sheets/mobile-technology-fact-sheet/

[3] http://oai.wsu.edu/teaching_resources/resources.html

out the internet, or Bill Colburn, a 65-year-old classmate and a "digital immigrant"[4] who had to learn the culture of social networking, one thing is crystal clear: Multitasking is rampant. Students acknowledged they spent more of their waking hours connected to their devices than disconnected. Some even admitted to checking their phones during the interview for this chapter, unable to sustain 20 minutes device free. And you, the reader, could easily be multitasking as you read these words.

For the digitally connected who have as much access to information as they want, any hour of the day, in most places in the world, it's important to ask—**how might technology be used to enhance student learning in higher education?**

Students aren't demanding lots of new smart boards, iPads, and other technology in the classroom as some might expect, although those are all nice to have. For the always connected, it's less about the hardware or new bright, shiny tools, and more about the access and experiences that technology enables. Students are deeply interested in how technology can improve learning in ways that are most important to them. Two critical themes:

1. Ability to manage their own learning

2. Participatory and practical experiences

The result? Technology is used to customize information in ways that are engaging, participatory, and fun. Enter curated edutainment, a concept where learning thrives inside and

---

[4] Ibid.

outside the classroom and where materials continue to connect over time and extend far beyond a single course. Content is thought of as an education and entertainment asset. Materials are developed and distributed to students through digital channels and existing platforms. In turn, students' needs are met; they'll have constant access to learning through the smartphones and laptops they're already glued to. And they'll increasingly be able to integrate learning into their always-on worlds.

Ability to Manage Their Own Learning

Every student is different. Are they visual learners or oral learners? Do they need to write everything down or listen to class recordings to memorize information? There is no one-size-fits-all model, and students don't want one. What they do want is the flexibility to design their own learning based on their strengths. Every single student interviewed for this chapter could easily identify what type of learner he or she is and how he or she retains information best.

Farrah Khaleghi, a psychology doctoral student at Pepperdine University, is prescriptive about how she needs to manage her learning: "I take notes, review and file my professor's PowerPoints, and then categorize related articles within my own organization system with searchable keyword tags."

Students are used to shaping experiences in their own lives. Whether it's their social-media profile, how they set up their calendars, or where they get their news, students are constantly designing information systems that work best for them. This translates directly to the university classroom.

Sean Brownlee, an Arabic studies graduate of the Defense Language Institute, says, "If I have the class agenda ahead of time, I have clarity of direction, and the time I spend preparing will build into what I learn in the next class." Students need access to course information and material upfront to be able to design a learning management system that works for them.

Doctoral student Khaleghi agrees: "It is really annoying when professors show articles or links and say I will post this after class, and then they either don't, or they wait for three or four days. It is really important to me that everything is posted before the class so I can save it and reference as I want to."

For military students, the stakes can be even higher. Brownlee says: "I have to prepare in advance, because it helps me develop the habit of always being prepared, which makes it easier to gain and retain knowledge. And I knew I had to manage my time extremely efficiently, again, why the habit part of learning was so important. I could not fall behind. If I failed my studies, and luckily I didn't, my job in the military would have changed completely, and not for the better."

Tom Patton, a recent international studies graduate of the University of Oregon said it boils down to maximizing value for time: "I want to know what I need to know before class, so I can go to class and have group discussions that aren't a regurgitation of information that I could have saved walking a mile through the rain and read at home."

Sakai, Blackboard, and iLearn are Learning Management Systems (LMS) that allow students to have full access to course information. Few students criticized the platforms themselves or complained about functionality, but they shared a sense of frustration in not having visibility into the requirements, expectations, materials, and deliverables in a course. Students are far more concerned about the content than the specifics of platforms. They're used to accessing multiple platforms. As long as everything course related is in one place and they have 24-hour access from any device, they're satisfied.

There are few moments in a day when students can't pull out their phone and get a quick answer, so knowing you may or may not have the course information you need when you need it creates anxiety for multi-taskers. Multitaskers survive and thrive when they 1) have access to endless information, anywhere, at any time, on any of their devices, and 2) can prioritize how they spend their time based on known expectations.

Students also want to make sure they are getting the most value out of their courses. Spending time trying to figure out how to get the basic information they need is time not spent doing the work that needs to be done, so they can catch the end of that football game. School is a part of what they do, and if they're using digital and social technology to drive pro-ductivity on the job and in their social lives, they want the same benefits at school.

Having access to information upfront drives efficiency and engagement.

Gone are the days when students needed to be in a library to access books or in a computer lab to write papers. Learning can happen anytime, anywhere, and is repeatable. Familiarity with new concepts before they are introduced allows students to plan better. They know much earlier how much time they need to invest based on their existing knowledge, strengths, and busy schedules.

Jelise Milani Baires, a business management junior at San Francisco State University and a busy mom says: "It's important to know what to expect, and you know a little about it. If I'm introduced to concepts before, I'm immediately more engaged. It helps with the experience and reduces anxiety because I can prep better."

The availability of materials to review in your own time also encourages collaboration amongst students. Says Khaleghi: "I learn most in presentations when I review material on my own time, then create a project with classmates, present a Power-Point to my classmates to capture feedback, and then have a Q&A discussion."

Patton agrees, "I loved having resources online before class. I could then use the internet, outside resources, or collaborate more with classmates to answer questions I had. Sometimes, we'd come to class as a group of students with questions. And that was extremely helpful in retaining information faster, because I could recognize what I didn't know before I sat down to write a paper or take a test."

Technology can support clarity of information not only when posted online but also during class itself. Robert Jordan, a business management senior at North Carolina State University, describes the benefits of smart screens especially in large lecture halls: "The professor can very easily write on a blank piece of paper, and it's projected on screen. It's very legible, I really like it. He or she can then write out full pages of paper, refer to different sheets, and it's easy to switch between projector and presentation; it's easier to follow and stay focused."

If students feel in control of their learning, there are multiple benefits, including increased motivation to do well. For students that manage their own learning and have been given the material and tools needed to do so, it becomes harder to blame a professor or group member for a lousy outcome. It also enables students to better plan their time to take more advantage of external resources. Instead of struggling to keep up and meet requirements, they're able to work ahead and learn information on their own time. Students are using class time, lectures, clubs, and other resources to reinforce or even practice new concepts.

The LMSs that exist today are platforms focused on individual classes. They are a filing cabinet for course information that dies at the end of a course. What students want are full learning centers where they can find what's most relevant from a pile of endless information, much as Google search works. They want to start with what is most engaging to them and build knowledge from there. What if different-but-related classes are connected together and you can easily move from basic to advanced topics, with endless lists of resources, practical ways to apply learning, and self-guided exercises? If a student is interested in a specific topic or area they have the tools to go deep, anytime, anywhere, on any device.

Students use digital technology to manage schedules, learn, share, play games, and collaborate. Why not repackage class information for distributions through the same devices in the same style students are consuming everything else in their lives? Having a database of information on all courses taken during an extended period of study opens up new opportunities to apply concepts over time.

Learning is not linear. Many students constantly find themselves going back to review, revisit, and make new connections. If students are attached to their devices all day, everyday, why not make it easy for them to access and manage their learning not just for next week's class, but next year?

Participatory and Practical Experiences

In an age where knowledge accumulation is not the end goal, students need to be increasingly savvy about how to access information, ask the right questions, and apply new concepts. The classroom is no longer a closed book, a singular chapter, but is quite literally a window into the world. With technology, outside ideas can be accessed in real-time to demonstrate the applications, challenges, and opportunities of a given topic; participatory learning can be activated.

With billions of videos on the internet and easily searchable platforms like You Tube, videos are increasingly part of the classroom experience. The human brain craves visual stimulus every 2-3 seconds[5], and videos offer an easy break in lectures. But students are critical; they want to know if the videos are fun to watch and if they support overall learning objectives.

Chloe Biren, an undeclared sophomore at Emory University explains: "When videos that are entertaining and describe

---

[5] Dr. Carmen Simon, Rexi Media.

what we're learning about in a new way, I'm highly engaged. When it's a boring video or something not relevant, I become disengaged and passive towards the material."

When asked about videos in the classroom, Baires lets out a long sigh. "Do you mean the super boring videos that come with the text books that have graphics from the 1990s? Or do you mean TED talks and entertaining, real-world videos?"

Baires continues: "I can't just memorize information, I have to understand it, get the concept down. Good videos can really help me understand information, especially if I don't understand the first time around. And I really enjoy the classes where there is a discussion after the video. The professor doesn't just assume you'll remember everything but asks questions and draws the information out of us. Then I really feel like I retain what I just learned."

Relevant videos that are used as tools to engage, excite, and motivate students or expose them to material from a new perspective accelerate learning. Active learning is the priority; videos can be a laugh-out-loud supporting partner but only if relevant. And depending on the course, no technology might be acceptable.

Biren describes her favorite class, which had no technology at all: "In my philosophy class my professor held us accountable for the reading, so I always prepared in advance. She was a smart and a great lecturer, made learning the material fun. Her classes were highly structured, so you knew exactly what to expect. She ran every class the same way. She would start with a broad overview of the reading, the class asked questions, and then she answered them. [There was] no technology—she wrote on a board. But I was highly engaged and I learned (and retained a lot of information) as a result."

Khaleghi shares her view: "Too much technology can feel like you're avoiding the discussion. If a professor is highly reliant on PowerPoint and showing videos, it can feel like you're not really engaging with the material. As a professional-degree student, I need to get good at the material, and that means discussing it a lot. That being said, it's hard to take a class seriously that uses no technology at all; it feels too out of touch with reality."

Technology also enables case studies and real-world examples to be easily and comprehensively brought into the classroom. It's how the material is curated that's important; the real measure of success for students is how these real-world applications contribute to overall learning.

Jordan describes his most memorable class at North Carolina State University: "The professor had an easy to follow lecture based on the readings I had prepared. He had examples from the book and real-world examples. I learned by taking notes, and I remember in this class my pen never stopped because there was so much exciting, new information from this combination of examples from the book, which I was already familiar with through the homework assignments, and real world applications."

A new way professors are driving participatory learning is using i-clickers[6], remote-control devices students use in the classroom to answer questions that measure in real time student participation and comprehension. Professors can

---

[6] www1.iclicker.com

immediately display results, record responses, and adjust materials based on classroom comprehension. Students will know if they are getting answers wrong and therefore missing concepts. Student reviews are mixed.

Jordan describes the use of i-clickers at NC State: "When I know i-clickers are being used, it definitely makes me go to class. It's a small device, very easy to forget at home, not fun when you do. I do find myself paying more attention in class, and it gives the professor a quick gauge if students are getting the concept. I find they're particularly useful in large lectures."

Khaleghi is pretty passionate in saying they don't work for graduate students: "In the classes we used clickers, they were really hard to get to work, and a lot of class time was spent troubleshooting the technology. Once we did get them working, they felt juvenile. I didn't feel like I was participating. It felt more like a barrier to learning, I was so focused on getting the clicker to work and what the clicker answer was (not the concept)."

The benefits of i-clickers are in the direct student and professor feedback. As a student you know if you're getting the concept the professor is teaching. However it's an extra device, not part of the tools and systems students have built across their laptops and mobile phones. And as a result, the technology feels clunky. It is not a seamless participatory experience, at least not yet.

Online Classes

Students are asking the same questions about online classes as they do about videos and clickers. Is the material engaging?

Interesting? Are there real-life examples? Am I inspired? Good online classes would be all of these things; bad ones become a tedious box-ticking exercise, quite literally in some cases.

Hatzistratis talks about the worst online course he's ever taken, it was a mandatory introduction-to-marketing course at San Francisco State University: "There is a quiz every two weeks, which is worth half of your grade. It's no news to anyone that all you have to do is copy and paste the questions in an internet search. For years students have been doing this; it's just way too easy."

Technology is being used to game the system in the same ways it's being used to drive deep learning. What becomes critical is that digital learning, in whatever form, is relevant, engaging, fun, and customizable to individual student strengths.

Patton really enjoyed his online classes and found himself wishing he could have taken even more: "By my senior year, a lot of my classes were super-redundant. The structure of an online class really works for me. I know upfront what I need to know for the week. There are resources to ask questions on the homework and quizzes every week. I was learning as I went versus cramming for a big midterm. As long as materials are helpful in their explanation, I learn really well working through the concepts on my own, trying to figure it out."

Technology is a critical driver of participatory and active learning, but striking the right balance between outside tools, videos, demonstrations, and traditional composition books, pens, paper, and lots of discussion is what most students want. No amount of technology will make up for a really exciting, engaging, knowledgeable professor who challenges students to think differently.

Monika Gupta, a recent MBA graduate of the University of Michigan, envisions collaboration in her ideal class: "There would be plenty of time to brainstorm and collaborate with fewer tight deadlines. You'd be challenged to use new tools and push yourself. You'd be designing solutions but also figuring out how to execute these new ideas. There would be moments when you needed to talk through things in real-time with no technology and times when you would need technology. Learning wouldn't be segmented; it would match the real world when sometimes you have technology to research, respond, solve, and sometimes you just have your words and a pen and paper."

When discussing with students what their dream class would be, few imagined a totally new system. Instead, like Gupta, they were looking at ways to improve or build upon current learning networks and spoke about their most engaging class, and how interactive learning models could be replicated to other areas of study.

Curated Edutainment

Its clear students want to manage and participate in their learning more directly than ever before. Accustomed to finding answers and designing experiences in their daily lives, students demand this same kind of interaction at school. They also recognize that being "learned" today is not memorizing information but being able to apply concepts to new situations, which requires real-world exposure and practice.

Technology is a critical enabler, but tools used must support the learning objectives of the students they support.

There is an increasing emphasis on content, which can be broken into different areas: information about the course itself, core concepts to the course, real-life use cases, and practical experiences. Content that is the most consumable is that which educates and entertains.

Curated edutainment is a way to collect all materials for a course, from requirements to use cases, and organize them in a way that is valuable and fun. It's critical that there is an endless supply of resources that build on each other and directions students can turn, as they manage their own learning and work through problems. Supported by time in the classroom, students are empowered with engaging materials that are distributed through the same devices and channels that are familiar to them.

Gamification could be one way to drive engagement in this edutainment model. Thinh Ta, a business management senior at San Francisco State whose family moved from Vietnam five years ago, had to learn an entire new education system. In thinking about his ideal class, he talks at length about gamification: "Make the class like a game with levels. Homework is 5 points, 5 knowledge points. If you have a lot of points, you'll gain a level. At first everyone does them all, monthly competition. I'd be engaged, I love games!"

It's critical to understand how students want to learn in today's ever-more connected world. They need flexibility and adaptability to access information and resources for self-guided learning; they need rich, engaging in-class experience where complex concepts are crystallized in practical ways; and they seek a vibrant learning community on and offline. Thinking about technology, not in terms of a single tool but instead as for a curated edutainment system that activates learning, is powerful and effective.

5 Ways To Accelerate Learning in a Digital World

1. Provide all course information upfront for anytime, anywhere access.

2. Curate course materials so students can learn (review) concepts at their own pace, in their own learning style.

3. Build in practical experiences and real-world case studies.

4. Experiment with content—don't be afraid to ditch the traditional PowerPoints, create a game, have fun, see what happens!

5. Connect concepts between courses and over an entire period of study; let course material live beyond a semester.

||||||||||||||||||||||||||||||||||||||||||||||||||||||||||||||||||||||||||||||||||||||||||||||||||||||||||||||||||||||||||||||||||||||||||||||||||||||||||||||||||||||||||||||||||||

CELENA APONTE currently designs and teaches "Creativity and Innovation" at San Francisco State University, a semester-long undergraduate course where students learn creative approaches to business problems.

Celena spent ten years representing some of the worlds' biggest entertainers learning, often from the frontline, how to find audiences and build stories. Currently, she's co-leading data strategy in Cisco's Americas Field Marketing where she's leveraging insights from data to customize customer marketing.

Celena has an MBA from the Middlebury Institute of International Studies and a BS in Communications from New York University.

Chapter 7

University Administration in the Digital Age

Chapter 7

University Administration in the Digital Age

By Mohammad Qayoumi

Overview

An innovative, highly skilled, and educated workforce has supplemented and sustained the United Stated during the last century. One of the drivers behind this phenomenon is the growth and demand for higher education. Today, there are more than 4,500 higher education institutions across the country with a total operating budget of more than a trillion dollars. It is safe to say that higher education has evolved into one of the most complex sectors of our economy.

Before one can address the importance of administration, it would be helpful to discuss the digital impact of technology on higher education from an administrator's perspective. Indeed, technology has moved university administration beyond automating basic administrative routines. We are now dealing with smart classrooms and a multitude of online course offerings, which force administrators to examine how faculty are compensated (rewarded) for changes in hours and skills sets. In addition, new learning management systems— ERP (Enterprise Resources Planning) approaches are replacing older processes. These new systems standardize systems and increase efficiency, but the implementation can be fraught with headaches.

One of the major impacts of the digital age is how organizations have moved from a scarcity of information to an almost unlimited abundance. Another impact is the hyperconnectivity that our students and professors expect. The pace of change is exponential, while typically organizations like universities have adapted to change at a linear pace at best. This means universities must develop more innovative ways to adjust processes, become more nimble, more efficient, and more technologically savvy, or fall behind. It also means creating a more digitally attuned learning environment. One of the most important roles for university administrators is to prepare and adjust the organizational culture to best respond, and even anticipate, changes in our transforming world. An administrator must move from merely solving day-to-day problems to imagining new possibilities and shift institutional paradigms to meet the demands of the digital age.

The Importance of Administration

Many important dimensions to higher education administration make it quite different from administration in other enterprises. First, the academic culture is primarily shaped by the way it deals with issues and challenges. Faced with an issue, this culture usually pauses and deliberates, and then deliberates again, but will not necessarily reach a definitive conclusion. This process is sacrosanct but inhibits moving forward. That is why for some in the academic sphere, no decision is ever complete, and the same issue may be revisited multiple times even after a course has been determined. Technology leadership is often the casualty, as it often gets crowded out by seemingly more important and immediate issues of the day. This approach is very contrary to the temperament of most administrators. One of the factors that reinforced this practice was that in the early years of higher education development, senior faculty members filled most administrative positions. That practice is still prevalent within many institutions for the majority of presidents, chancellors, and almost all provost positions.

The second fundamental and philosophical difference is the nature of many not-for-profit organizations, which constitutes the vast majority of higher education institutions with the exception of for-profit entities that have emerged within the past few decades. For-profit corporations provide a defined set of products and services to their customers and maximize the return on investment (ROI) for their stockholders. These entities are always attempting to find ways to reduce costs by introducing new technologies and innovative approaches to contain cost. As the cost of operation is reduced, the additional margin is used to reinvest in expanding the enterprise, increase dividends to stockholders, pass on the savings to the customers, or some combinations of the three. By contrast, higher education institutions are value-maximization enterprises given the fixed amount of resources they have at hand. So, if the cost of operation is reduced using new processes or technologies, the savings is used to add more services to enhance the mission such as investing in new educational offerings, research activities, etc. As costs increase, universities try to reduce their costs modestly, or they pass on the extra cost in the form of increased fees and tuition. Because of this asymmetry, cost control is more complex in higher education.

Key Administrative Functions

Although every higher education institution may have a unique organizational structure, there are some key similarities. For many, the administration structure is divided into four major divisions namely:

- Academic affairs
- Business and administrative affairs
- Student services
- University advancement

The bulk of the university administration is in the business and administrative division, which may include the following key functional areas:

- Business and finance
- Facilities maintenance and plant operations
- Human resources
- Procurement and purchasing
- Risk management
- Public safety
- Information technology (IT)

Another major administrative function within universities involves managing financial aid. Given the large amounts of federal, state, and local funds they handle, university administrators must have a great understanding of this function. In addition, this area is one of the highly regulated functions within a plethora of federal, state, and local rules.

Information Technology Concerns in the Digital Age

The strategic importance of information technology is hard to overestimate in every enterprise, and higher education is no exception. A couple of decades ago, IT was only a small percentage of a university's budget. In the past decade, IT has increased to more than 7% of the budget for many institutions. In the digital age, the strategic role of IT is gaining more attention. Traditionally, higher education, like many other industries, viewed IT as automation of manual processes. That is why the overwhelming implementation of IT applications were focused in automating many administrative processes such as payroll and other financial services, maintenance and operations, student admissions and records, etc. With the introduction of ERPs (Enterprise Resource Management) and web-based applications, administrators began to see the value of integration to form the basis for decision-support systems.

Also, with the proliferation of mobile systems and the expectation of connectivity anywhere, the IT function at universities has gained more importance. First, increasing importance is attached to having robust IT infrastructure on a 24/7 basis. Every person associated with the university expects to have connectivity at anytime and anywhere. What complicates this requirement is the insatiable appetite for more bandwidth. Consequently, expanding and maintaining high-speed networks is an ongoing challenge of the administration at every university. These concerns also incorporate addressing cyber security, confidentiality, and access.

There are a number of unique challenges in managing IT networks within the university structure. Unlike corporations that can prescribe what devices employees can utilize or prohibit employees from bringing any personal devices to the company, many university faculties believe they have the right to bring and utilize any device they desire and that the university must support it. In addition, some faculties continue running older versions of software without understanding that security patches are necessary and often conflict with older versions of software. In addition, almost every student brings his or her own device, which adds even more complexity to our university IT systems. Finally, another relevant issue is providing adequate training opportunities for all users, which can translate into a significant ongoing expense.

Risk Management

As complex enterprises, universities require risk management, and the responsibility for managing risk lies squarely on the shoulders of university administration. Given the numerous and interrelated processes in a university, the failure of one or more key operations could impede the mission fulfillment of the institution. There are numerous ongoing and one-time-event risk elements that a university has to take into account. These range from natural threats such as floods, earthquakes, tsunamis, hurricanes, and tornados, to system malfunctions or failures such as power outages, equipment breakdowns, computer crashes, or human-made threats such as sabotage, cyber attacks, fraud, acts of terrorism, etc. In the last decade, risk assessment has grown to include many information technology issues.

The first step in managing risk is developing a better understanding of risk. Risk is commonly referred to as an undesirable or unfavorable outcome that happens at some time in the future. This implies two related issues, namely the likelihood of an undesirable occurrence and the negative impact that may be due to that undesirable occurrence. The interaction of these two factors and their associated probabilities determine the risk. An alternate way to define risk is to view it as the collective effects of three elements, namely threats, vulnerabilities, and impacts. The threat refers to the likelihood of an occurrence due to a system or process weakness. Vulnerability refers to a system or process weakness that could be exploited by the threat. Finally, impact is the negative result that may happen because of the threat. Risk is the multiplication of these three factors.

It is important to note that since technology has permeated almost all areas of a university enterprise, each one of these areas have substantial technological risks associated with them. Some of the key risk factors are below:

Strategic Risk

- Long-term enrollment projections
- Potential demographic changes
- Major shifts in service areas
- Organizational image, brand, and reputation
- Major and impactful technology changes
- Significant shifts in delivery of instruction
- Possible competition from similar institutions
- Impact of for-profit universities
- The rise of MOOCs (Massive Open Online Courses)
- Governance and unionization issues
- Long-term funding trends

Legal Risk

- Major shifts in federal, state, or local regulations
- Awareness, understanding, and appropriate interpretation of existing laws
- Having a systematic plan for compliance
- Developing ongoing training program for everyone—especially in cyber security awareness
- Understanding and applying best practices towards securing records, identities, and other forms of personal information
- Conducting periodic audits

Financial Risk

- Accuracy and adequacy of financial statements
- Instituting adequate financial and system controls
- Assuring financial integrity of financial and personal information
- Segregation of duties of key staff involved in financial processes
- Effective investment and endowment management
- Effective payroll system and payment disbursement
- Inventory management for capital equipment
- Control of major financial processes, i.e. account receivables, procurement, account payables, cash flow, etc.

Operational Risk

This risk category covers largely the operational issues relating to major functions of the university. Key examples of these risks are briefly stated below for major functional areas:

- Academic Programs: academic freedom; curricular control and monitoring; implementing academic policies, faculty reviews, tenure, promotion; etc.

- Human Resources: hiring policies for faculty and staff; employee relations factors such as disciplines and grievances; classification and employee appraisal; benefit management including the protection of vital records

- Facilities Operations and Management: major utilities interruptions; building and premise security (both physical and virtual) issues; accessibility issues including ADA (Americans with Disabilities Act) requirements; etc.

- Environmental Health and Safety: hazardous materials and waste management; workers' safety; building and grounds safety; disaster preparedness; etc.

- Student Admission and Records: confidentiality of student records; admission policies, standards, and enrollment management; financial aid award and disbursement, etc.

- Information Management: Ensuring data integrity, security, and confidentiality; hardware reliability and obsolescence; backup and recovery, cyber security; etc.

- Athletics: compliance with National Collegiate Athletic Association (NCAA) rules and with Title IX of the 1972 U.S. Education Amendments, which protect people from sex discrimination in education programs and activities receiving federal financial assistance; recruitment, retention, and graduation of athletes; budget management and community support; institutional brand and image, etc.

- Sponsored Research: intellectual property issues; compliance especially relating to key federal agencies such as the Government Accountability Office and Office of Management and Budget; indirect cost calculations and disbursement methodology for federal aid; reporting to sponsoring agencies and project management; etc.

- Miscellaneous areas such as auxiliaries operations: TV and radio station operation; children and day care services; international partnerships, public/private partnerships; etc.

Looking at the above long list of possible risk categories it is natural to feel overwhelmed. There are a number of ways to address risk. One approach is to develop a two-by-two matrix where one axis will represent the frequency of occurrence and the second will represent the impact. By conducting this exercise, we get four possible buckets: low frequency of occurrence with low impact, low frequency of occurrence with high impact, high frequency of occurrence with low impact, and high frequency of occurrence with high impact. The next step is to divide all risks into these four categories. This gives one the opportunity to develop a different approach for each risk category.

The Cost of Education

There have been sizable increases in the cost of higher education for the past three decades. Between 1986-87 and 1996-97, the tuition at public universities increased by 20% and at private universities, by 31%. Concerns about the size of these increases was articulated very early in 1999 by James F. Carlin, a former chair of the Massachusetts Board of Education and former trustee of the University of Massachusetts, in an article titled "Restoring Sanity to an Academic World Gone Mad."[1]

By the beginning of 2010, the average tuition at public universities reached $12,000, and it was $35,000 at private universities. One of the natural consequences of tuition increases was the meteoric rise in total student loans to more than a trillion dollars, an amount higher than U.S. credit card debt.[2] Policy makers and the general public became sufficiently concerned that tuition and fee increases now face strong opposition in many states. Similarly, the allocations that federal and state governments are willing to make to colleges and universities are not keeping up with general cost escalations.

The aforementioned factors are creating new and unique challenges for higher education administrators. Over the course of the last decade, university administrators have introduced new technologies, especially in the IT area, in an effort to enhance efficiency and reduce the costs of many administrative functions. However, in most universities roughly 80% of expenditures are directly related to the delivery of instruction. Most institutions have tried to contain this cost by increasing class sizes or by using more teaching assistants or lecturers as instructors. Although these efforts have reduced expenses, in many cases they are not enough to contain all cost pressures.

---

[1] Carlin, J., "Restoring Sanity to an Academic World Gone Mad" *The Chronicle of Higher Education,* Nov 4, 1999, A76

[2] "Student Debt Exceeds One Trillion Dollars," NPR, April 24, 2012. www.npr.org/2012/04/24/151305380/student-loan-debt-exceeds-one-trillion-dollars

The road forward is fraught with risky challenges and potential opportunities, thus defining the importance of learning more about the role of the administrator.

A key higher education stakeholder is state government. Until 1980, states provided significantly larger percentages of higher education funds. During that period in many states, roughly 60% to 85% of public higher education funding was provided by state appropriations. As a result, state legislators and governors had a tremendous influence over these institutions. Although public higher education institutions (especially those set up as land-grant institutions) have a lot more freedom than state agencies, and are governed by independent boards of trustees, in most cases the board members are selected by a state governor and confirmed by legislators. In addition, a number of senior public officers are members of these boards.

Since 1980, state appropriations have followed a monotonically downward trend. In good economic times public universities experienced upticks in state appropriations in almost all cases, but the increases were too small to compensate for the loss of resources during the lean years. An analysis published in February 2012 in the research newsletter *Postsecondary Education Opportunity* best articulates this drop in state support. In an article entitled "The Race to Zero," the researchers report that they plotted state-appropriation reductions for public higher education in every state from 1980 to 2012 and extrapolated from that data, how long it would take for state support to disappear.[3]

---

[3] "The Race to Zero," *Postsecondary Education Opportunity,* February 2012, www.postsecondary.org/commondetail.asp?id=1625

According to this report, if the aforementioned downward trends continue at the same pace, state funding will drop to zero in Colorado within the next decade. The next state to follow suit would be Alaska, and California would hit zero by 2052. By the end of this century, the state funding of an additional 24 states would be zero, and only 10 states would continue their support for higher education. Some have compared the trend line on state funding to an EKG reading for a person who is going to have a heart attack. Today, state appropriations typically account for 15% to 45% of university budgets.

In reaction to reductions in the proportion of state funding, many universities tried to cut costs and increase tuition and fees. That has been the principal reason for increases in tuition above the inflation rate for public universities since the mid 1980s. As mentioned earlier, many students ended up borrowing more funds, which resulted in an unprecedented high level of student debt. Some have argued, albeit unsuccessfully, that when a state was providing almost all the financial support, it was justified in exerting strong control over its public universities; however, as state support diminishes, the universities should be awarded more autonomy.

As colleges seek ways to make up for reductions in State spending, it is not surprising, one of the newest fee categories is a "technology fee" that provides wired and wireless broadband as well as other forms of technology equipment and services.

The Acropolis vs. the Agora

Within a university environment, there is fundamental cultural difference between the academic areas and the administration. The dominant culture of academia is built on collegiality and shared governance. This explains the relationship between the administration and the faculty in giving input and advice on critical institutional decisions. Moreover, certain functions such as the curriculum, the academic calendar, policies on recruitment and evaluation of senior administrators are the purview of the faculty. Therefore, unlike most other industries the issues of final authority and responsibility are more complex in the life of a university. The relationship between authority and responsibility rests in a collaborative process in most situations. This shared governance requires a close relationship between the faculty and administration that is based upon a transparent system.

One of the complicating factors in a shared-governance environment is the introduction of collective bargaining. In other words, on campuses where faculty organize and negotiate a union contract with management, shared governance dynamics can become even more complicated. This often means an administrator needs to spend a considerable amount of time communicating his or her position to numerous individuals and constituencies before certain decisions can be finalized. For example, online teaching and distance learning often require changes in a faculty's load level and overall working conditions. Even when all parties are in general agreement, the devil is always in the details, and collective bargaining is but one example.

During the past couple of decades, as the public has demanded more accountability from public higher education institutions, many state legislatures have begun requiring specific measures of outcomes. In their rhetoric, hardly anyone opposes these measurements, but such metrics represent a fundamental paradigm shift that many higher education institutions find difficult. Traditionally, college and university budgets tracked inputs, not outputs. Moreover, there were usually minimal links between plans and budgets. In an effort to introduce modest levels of efficiency improvements these institutions have begun comparing their costs to similar higher education institutions.

This practice contrasts, however, with a performance orientation based on outcome-focused budgeting and one where plans drive budgets. In a performance-based environment, measures and metrics are outputs and outcome-based, and building a robust organization assessment model is an absolute necessity. Rather than mere cost comparisons, organizations embark on formal and informal benchmarking. The key reason why benchmarking can provide more breakthrough ideas is that it focuses attention on best-in-class organizations rather than on comparative costs that keep everyone's attention focused on averages.

Conclusion

There is hardly an administrator who does not recognize the need to adopt new technology applications in the learning environment as well as invest in the fast-growing digital infrastructure. Knowing where to go is far easier than getting there. With all its strengths and time-tested governance, the collegial model for governing almost always ensures slow-moving policies and procedures. There is also a painful recognition that if higher education does not move more quickly, other institutions—other nonprofit organizations along with for-profit organizations including some well-known corporations—will fill the growing gap. Technology in academia has already made some significant advances regarding smarter classrooms, improved wireless communications, faster and more secure networks, as well as advanced video-rich learning management systems. There is no doubt; technology will play an increasing and evermore-important role in every aspect of college and university life.

‖‖‖

MOHAMMAD QAYOUMI is the 28th president and a professor of electrical engineering at San Jose State University. He holds a bachelor's degree in electrical engineering from the American University of Beirut and four degrees from the University of Cincinnati: master's degrees in business administration, nuclear engineering, and electrical and computer engineering, and a doctorate in electrical engineering. He has more than 37 years of engineering and administrative experience in several universities. He has also published eight books and more than 100 articles and chapters in books. He is a licensed professional engineer and a certified management accountant. A senior member of IEEE and Senior Fellow of the California Council on Science and Technology, he also chairs cyber security and campus resilience for the U.S. Department of Homeland Security. He was named to the Carnegie Corporation's list of "Great Immigrants: Pride of America."

Chapter 8

Corporate Action and Corporate Responsibility in the Corporate Age

Chapter 8

Corporate Action and Corporate Responsibility in the Digital Age

By Ronda Mosley

The sobering statistics are in. In the current job market, there are two to three million unfilled positions because companies cannot find workers with basic technical skills. We will have 10 million such openings before the end of the decade.[1] The corporate sector needs a skilled workplace that mirrors the digital age marketplace. The corporate sector also needs a diverse skilled workforce to imagine, to innovate, to collaborate, to understand, to build, to manage, to sell, to protect (cybersecurity), and to repair the products that everyone will utilize in the digital age. Corporations also need to benefit themselves while also benefiting society.

These sentences hide a complicated back-story. Today, competencies for innovation are scattered across a wider swath of the economy.[2] There is a growing disconnect between our current educational system and the workers that it produces and the increasing technical needs that stretch across the vast corporate sector.

---

[1] Kelly, Brian. "What is STEM and Why We Care," *U.S. News and World Report,* 2012.

[2] Carnevale, Anthony. STEM. Georgetown University Center on Education and the Workforce, 2010.

Former President Clinton's secretary of education, Richard Riley, summed up this need for innovation to drive our future when he predicted what is now occurring. "The jobs in the greatest demand in the future don't exist and will require workers to use technologies that have not yet been invented to solve problems that we don't yet even know are problems.[3]

This disconnect is forcing meaningful conversation and urgent action by corporations—their very livelihoods depend on their continued ability to be nimble, to build specific business cases, and to bring resources to attack this educational and technical deficit. The outcome of this corporate action means filling much-needed technical jobs, sparking innovation, increasing connectivity, and igniting the global economy. This conversation, as the corporate sector understands, starts with science, technology, engineering, and math (STEM) education, but does not stop there. This action requires emphasized refocus and resources to fill the needs of a diverse digital age workforce—STEM Plus or STE**A**M (science, technology, engineering, **art,** and math).

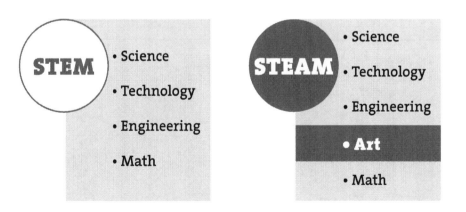

[3] White, Harvey. Our education System is not so much "Broken"—as it is Totally Outdated!, http://steam-notstem.com

In today's competitive world, our schools and universities need to teach not only how to find facts but what to do with these facts. We must teach our students how to synthesize, how to inter-relate, how to build systems and processes based on the acquired facts, and how to question individual facts by seeing how they fit with more complex constellations of facts. We need to teach how to deal with ambiguities and nuances—how to think creatively and how to construct or deal with abstract issues. These skills build a base for creativity and teach innovation. The rote learning of facts, which are soon forgotten but that students know can easily be reacquired if ever needed, is not consistent with what either students or business need to be successful in today's world.[4] Corporations are aware of this need. They are also aware that their employees need these specialized skills to meet future technical applications and want to work with schools and universities to support programs that teach innovation and creativity. Unfortunately, schools move more slowly than some would like. While corporate America continues to support higher education in many ways—its leaders realize corporations must develop and support their own initiatives too.

A wonderful real-world example of this emphasis on STEAM learning is with the late Steve Jobs. Jobs dropped out of Reed College his first year, but his interest in the liberal arts did not wane. He audited classes in calligraphy, and the sense of design he learned there found its way into the Macintosh environment. Even more important, Jobs became convinced that the greatest achievements of his businesses would take place when computer scientists worked alongside artists and

---

[4] White, Harvey. "Our education System is not so much broken—as it is Totally Outdated!," http://steam-notstem.com

designers, and he designed his workplaces so that people with these diverse intellects would be forced to rub shoulders. "One of the greatest achievements at Pixar was that we brought these two cultures together and got them working side by side," Jobs said in 2003.[5] Here is what Jobs explained when he rolled out the iPad 2: "It is in Apple's DNA that technology alone is not enough. It is technology married with liberal arts, married with humanities, that yields the results that make our hearts sing."[6]

"STEM,"a landmark 2010 study by Georgetown University Center on Education and the Workforce, reports, "Through 2018, the share of STEM occupations in the economy will grow to 5% up from 4.4% in 2005—a growth in the number of STEM jobs from 6.8 million to 8 million by 2018." This report further states that "STEM occupations will grow far more quickly than the economy as a whole (17% versus 10%), and will be the second-fastest growing occupational cluster, after healthcare occupations."[7] This extensive and often-referred-to study underscores the link between STEM Plus, or STEAM, education to fill needed positions (advanced manufacturing, utilities and transportation, mining, computer sciences, and other technology-driven industries) and the continued economic growth and prosperity of the U.S. economy.

This study also points out more and more occupations will require STEAM competencies for all levels of employees. The

---

[5] Richard Hurley. "Beyond STEM: Educating a Workforce of Thinkers and Doers," *Business Horizon Quarterly.*

[6] *The New Yorker* file://localhost/, http/:www.newyorker.com:online:blogs:newsdesk:2011:10:steve-jobs-pixar

[7] Carnevale, Anthony. STEM. Georgetown University Center on Education and the Workforce, 2010.

digital-age workforce goes beyond just needing more engineers and scientists; it must have competencies that have a much broader reach, including finance, arts and humanities, business, law, and healthcare and social interests. Going forward, we will need more workers with STEM Plus, or STEAM, competencies. Companies want workers who can brainstorm, problem-solve, collaborate creatively, and contribute/communicate new ideas.[8] Our traditional STEM approach needs modification to fit the demands of this changing landscape, and the corporate sector is leading the charge.

There are exciting initiatives already underway that companies large and small across the country are leading and investing in with better trained teachers to motivate students (especially girls and minorities) to study science and math and arts and humanities to build skill sets that employers require in an increasing technically connected world. These investments are focusing on all aspects of student and adult education—K-12, career centers, community colleges, and university programming. Below are just a few examples of corporate investment and action that are contributing to and expanding STEM and STEAM programming to educate the 21st century workforce.

■ Intel CEO Brian Krzanich recently announced that he would dedicate $300 million to sponsor STEM education in K-12 classes and universities, with a focus on underserved regions. The money is part of a broader effort to boost diversity among its workforce and will fund recruiting, training, and investments in female and

---

[8] Tarnoff, John. STEM to STEAM. http://steam-notstem.com/articles

minority-owned startups, along with education.[9] Intel also has a successful *Teach Program,* reaching 10 million teachers in 70 countries. In the United States, Intel® Teach helps K-12 teachers deepen their knowledge of 21st century learning concepts. Program courses show teachers how to engage students with digital learning, focusing on their students' problem-solving, critical-thinking, and collaboration skills—precisely the ones required in today's high-tech, networked society.[10]

▪ The Cisco Networking Academy Program is a novel idea where students worldwide gain the skills needed to build, design, and maintain computer networks, improving their career prospects while filling the global demand for networking professionals. With 9,000 academies in 170 countries, this Networking Academy helps individuals prepare for industry-recognized certifications, entry-level information, and communication technology (ICT) careers in virtually every type of industry. Students develop foundational skills in ICT while acquiring vital 21st century career skills in problem solving, collaboration, and critical thinking.

The Cisco Networking Academy uses a public-private partnership model to create the "world's largest classroom." Cisco collaborates with educational institutions, nonprofits, nongovernmental organizations, and community centers that provide classroom space, computer lab equipment, and qualified instructors.

---

[9] Michal Lev-Ram. "The Business Case for STEM Education," *Fortune.*com 2015.

[10] http://www.intel.com

Cisco provides online curricula, virtual learning tools, instructional support, teacher training, and professional development opportunities for instructors.[11]

- Another excellent example of corporate investment and action is the Ford Motor Company's Next Generation Learning (FORD NGL) program that mobilizes educators, employers, and community leaders to develop a new generation of employees who will graduate career-ready. Ford NGL improves teaching and learning, promotes the development of career and interest-themed high schools to better serve students and align business and civic engagement in education to improve student and workforce outcomes.

- The company 3M has just launched a very interesting $400,000 corporate giving program geared towards encouraging students to keep sustainability (energy and environmental fields) open as a career option. 3M explains this program as follows: "Over the long run programs that help guide early science, technology, engineering, and math (STEM) education along a sustainability track could have a significant impact on the future viability of green-transitioning companies like 3M, which are depending on the next generation of innovators to keep them competitive in a world of shrinking resources."

- General Electric (GE) has a new initiative involving training cybersecurity experts. The Information Security Technology Center links potential employees with

---

[11] http://www.cisco.com/web/learning/netacad/index.html

industry leaders who spark imaginative ideas and inspire collaboration and innovation. Nowhere else will you experience the groundbreaking innovation inspired by our development-focused culture. GE is reimagining and reinventing itself to meet the demands of the digital age—its web site touts, "Join us at the new GE."

■ The Exxon Mobile Foundation just announced a $520,000 grant to the National Action Council for Minority Engineers, Inc. (NACME). The council's focus is to introduce the field of engineering and career opportunities in engineering to underrepresented students, including African American, American Indian, and Latino women and men. According to research conducted by NACME, only 4% of ethnic minority students leave high school with the skills necessary to pursue engineering degrees.[12]

■ The Boeing Company makes a variety of investments in education throughout its service territory. Its philosophy is, "if we provide lifelong arts and cultural experiences, individuals will develop an appreciation for different perspectives, deepen their critical and creative thinking, and be better prepared to excel in work and life." The goal of Boeing's arts investment is to engage communities to participate in arts and cultural experiences in order to broaden their perspectives, nurture creativity, and produce a multidisciplinary workforce prepared to solve complex issues. The

---

[12] http://stemgrants.com/exxon-mobile-grant-delivers-520-grant-tonacme/

Boeing Company's arts investments foster creative expression, celebrate diverse cultures, stimulate civic dialogue, and strengthen communities.[13]

■ The Bayer USA Foundation, the philanthropic arm of Bayer Corporation, has announced a $540,000 grant to California State University, East Bay to support the creation of a Center for STEM education. The three-year grant will also establish the Bayer Executive Directorship to lead the center, and allow the school to expand regional teacher development programs for STEM subjects.[14]

■ IBM launched its Pathways in Technology Early College High School, or P-TECH, in Brooklyn, New York, where IBMers mentor students. This educational model for grades 9-14 leads to an associate degree in applied science to help prepare successful students to enter the workforce or complete a college degree. The P-TECH model is expanding throughout New York State to Chicago and other cities across the United States.

Corporate Social Responsibility

Another interesting question arises when one asks, "How can corporations meet their own internal needs (a diverse skilled workforce to imagine, to innovate, to collaborate, to understand, to build, to manage, to sell, to protect, and to repair the products that everyone will utilize in the digital age) while also serving the needs of the community and the

[13] http://www.boeing.com
[14] http://www20.csueastbay.edu/news

environment?" This is another interesting aspect of corporate sector action called corporate social responsibility.

Corporate responsibility has a wide variety of meanings, but
one of the most comprehensive and succinct descriptions
comes from the International Chamber of Commerce (ICC),
"Corporate responsibility is the commitment by companies to
manage their activities in a responsible way. More broadly,
corporate responsibility includes efforts by business to contribute to the society in which it operates."

Companies wield vast power within and around their communities, and across the national and global economy. Many corporations are using this power and devoting time and money
in environmental and community service initiatives, to benefit
their employees, customers, and the community at large.[15]
Smart corporations know that reinvestment into communities
and protecting the environment make great business sense.

Below are excellent examples of corporate responsibility programs resulting in real action. These companies are creating
programs that promote literacy and accessibility and afford-
ability of technology that actually encourage and promote
technology use and learning. All these programs also contribute to developing the next generations of technical workers.

- Comcast is offering a program entitled "Internet Es-
  sentials," which offers low-cost Internet service, computer equipment, and free digital literacy training to
  families with at least one child eligible to participate in
  the National School Lunch Program. The goal of this

---

[15] http://www.investopedia.com/terms

initiative is to bring more families online to begin to bridge the digital divide. This program also includes access to free Internet training—online, in print, and in person for the entire family.

- Intel has unveiled a new Classmate Notebook PC that is faster than its predecessors and features a touch screen for easier use. "This is a netbook specifically designed for kids," says Jeff Galinovsky, "Intel's regional manager for the Classmate PC. Computers used in the workplace are not suited for the classroom because in most cases they're fragile and too big for elementary and middle school students' desks," says Tony Salvadore, a senior principal engineer with Intel, who is also a psychologist and anthropologist. "Computing helped transform the way corporations work." Now it is time for them to do the same for education, he adds. The upgraded Classmate, now more efficient, faster, and with a longer battery life, also drew the attention of teachers in the U.S. and other developed countries. Classmates are "kid-friendly," Galinovsky says, adding that each has a carrying handle and a water-resistant keyboard. The Classmate's exterior is also made of tough plastic and can be dropped as far as two feet without serious damage. Intel and its partners developed the tablet model; because it is easier to use and carry, as opposed to the more conventional clamshell laptop design, which is more difficult to use when being held in one hand. The tablet model also has a thick touch screen so that a student can rest his or her hand on the screen while writing with a stylus.[16]

---

[16] Greenemeier, Larry. "New Tech Makes Classroom Computers a Reality Worldwide," *Scientific American.*

■ In September 2012, Microsoft refocused much of its efforts around creating opportunities for youth by launching Microsoft YouthSpark, a major initiative to connect hundreds of millions of youth with opportunities for education, employment, and entrepreneurship. The company is working to bridge the opportunity divide that separates youth who have opportunities from those who do not, with the goal of helping young people secure their individual futures and also the future of our global economy, reports Dan Bross, Microsoft's senior director of citizenship and public affairs.

■ Facebook and its leader Mark Zuckerberg have teamed with a number of organizations and corporations to launch *Internet.org.* According to Zuckerberg, the goal of Internet.org is to make affordable access to basic internet services available to every person in the world.

■ Many people take their computers, smartphones, and tablets for granted, but for those with disabilities, using these technologies can present significant challenges. Accessibility Partners works with private and public IT manufacturing companies, federal agencies, and other organizations to test and review products that make information technology accessible to individuals with a variety of disabilities. More than 70% of the company's employees have disabilities themselves, so the company promotes disability advocacy in all of its operations.[17]

---

[17] http://www.businessnewsdaily.com/5499-examples-socially-responsible-businesses.html

- TechSoup is an all-volunteer organization that has teamed with Adobe to provide new cloud-based products free to libraries and other nonprofit organizations. TechSoup has also teamed with Microsoft to create a software donation program that provides a wide variety of software to nonprofits, charities, faith-based organizations, and public libraries throughout the United States.

- Procter & Gamble focuses on helping children in need around the world. Since 2007, P&G has improved the lives of more than 210 million children through initiatives such as Protecting Futures, which helps vulnerable girls stay in school, and Hope Schools, which increases access to education in rural areas of China. "We see programs like Protecting Futures as an investment in the future that helps both children and communities thrive," says Jeff Roy, Procter & Gamble's media relations manager.[18]

- Dell is working with organizations around the world to close the learning gap for students that may not have access to quality education tools. Dell provides grants and technology and assigns a local Dell "Champion" to manage the deployment and upkeep of Dell systems and solutions. Local team members volunteer their time to support the organization's needs. Dell also addresses any basic or community needs that might hamper a child's ability to learn, such as food or

---

[18]http://www.forbes.com/sites/csr/2011/04/26/the-five-elements-of-the-best-csr-programs/

security. This shared responsibility between Dell and the community—supported by Dell volunteers—brings about real learning opportunities and change.[19]

■ Through its "World Ahead 1Mx15 Health Program," Intel aims to provide technical training to one million health-care workers in developing countries by the end of 2015.

■ Google has developed its Google Person Finder web application that allows individuals to post and search for friends and relatives following emergencies (such as the Boston Marathon bombing). The application is configured to permit nonprofits and government agencies to contribute and receive data. Following the 2010 Haiti earthquake, Google shared mapping data with the United Nations and other relief agencies.[20]

According to Bill Gates, former chairman and chief software architect of Microsoft Corporation, USA, "In an increasingly wired world, the roles of corporate manager and public citizen cannot be separated. A firm like Microsoft is judged on the skills of its employees, meaning issues such as job training and educational reform are now competitive as well as social factors, as the public expects business leaders to focus on issues that are legitimately connected to their economic responsibilities."[21]

---

[19] http://www.dell.com/learn/us/en/uscorp1/power-possible-learning

[20] http://www.ssireview.org/blog/entry/what_does_corporate_social_responsibility_mean_for_the_technology_sector, *Stanford Social innovation Review*

[21] http://info.worldbank.org/etools/docs/library/57494/saswati-paper.pdf

The business case for engaging in corporate social responsibility is clear and unmistakable. Billions are at stake if fast and large-scale action is not taken.

As consumers' awareness about global social issues continues to grow, so does the importance these customers place on corporate responsibility programs. "Technology has brought global connectivity and enabled advocacy and awareness for social situations that were once obscure," said Alexis Magnan-Callaway, whose fashion company Pax Cult donates 10% of its profits to an organization of each customer's choice. "Millennials are redefining what it means to connect and give back through this technology. It is not just about having a recycling program or sustainable products. People want to feel good about what their dollar is doing."[22]

Consumers are not the only ones who are drawn to businesses that give back. Susan Cooney, founder of crowdfunding philanthropy platform Givelocity, said that a company's corporate responsibility strategy is a big factor in where today's top talent chooses to work.

"The next generation of employees is seeking out employers that are focused on the triple bottom line: people, planet, and revenue," Cooney told *Business News Daily*. "Coming out of the recession, corporate revenue has been getting stronger. Companies are encouraged to put that increased profit into programs that give back."[23]

---

[22] http://www.businessnewsdaily.com/4679-corporate-social-responsibility. html, *Business News Daily*

[23] Ibid.

The outcome of this comprehensive corporate action means filling much-needed technical jobs, sparking innovation, increasing connectivity, and igniting the global economy. This is a win-win opportunity for communities across the world.

|||||||||||||||||||||||||||||||||||||||||||||||||||||||||||||||||||||||||||||||||||||||||||||||||||||||||||||||||||||||||||||||||||||||||||||||||||||||

RONDA MOSLEY, came to Public Technology Institute (PTI) in 1998 as Environmental Director and currently serves as Deputy Executive Director for Research and Government Services. Ms. Mosley has more than 25 years of professional experience. She has interdisciplinary academic training in energy, environmental issues, business administration, and technology implementation and deployment. She has pursued opportunities in both the United States and Latin America to broaden her understanding of cross-cultural issues, international policies, and their impact on program implementation.

Throughout the past seven years, under the auspices of PTI, Ms. Mosley has led or been the lead subcontractor in two groundbreaking multimillion-dollar projects designed to assist local governments produce energy assurance plans. These projects culminated in her co-authoring, *Local Government Energy Assurance Guidelines (Version I)* in 2009, and *Local Government Energy Assurance Guidelines (Version II)* in 2011.

Chapter 9

Parables, Brains, Campfires and Learning Design

Chapter 9

Parables, Brains, Campfires and Learning Design

By Raymond Smith and Stephen Wunderli

The way information is packaged and distributed has changed so much in the last two decades that it's easy to confuse dissemination with learning. Surrounded by more information doesn't necessarily make us smarter. We still have to determine what information is relevant, process it, own it, and use it.

We may no longer live in caves, but our brain processes have not changed much since those days huddled around the campfire. So, while there is much hype about new ways of learning—how we have a diminished attention span, and how we suddenly and magically developed the ability to multi-task—truth is, the way we learn has not actually changed much since the those early days. Current research explores how we process sensory inputs and how that processing interacts with what is now referred to as "working" and "long-term memory." Brain science research reveals that while we can multi-task, we do not do it very well, and that what appears to be a diminished attention span, is actually a brain on overload, distracted by all the information and stimulation in our digital world that bombards our senses—so much so that we have problems sorting out what is important and what is not.

Turns out, sitting around a campfire, telling stories, interacting with peers, using a few simple visual aids (cave paintings), and old-fashioned trial and error are still very effective ways to learn.

Can we improve upon that model in the new digital age? Certainly.

What has evolved is the nature of the campfire: how we gather, and how we exchange information and incorporate it into our lives.

If the digital revolution were only about devices and programs and the economy of mass teaching, the results are very disappointing. Take Massive Open Online Courses (MOOCs) for example, the first brave shot at reaching the masses that reside outside the classroom. The attrition rate for MOOCs can be up to 96%. While some academics point to a success rate enjoyed by those who did manage to complete the course, we're still talking about the majority of learners having dropped out. It's easy to discard MOOCs altogether with findings like these; but as is with any revolution, the first approach is rarely exactly right. Yet, without that first approach, we wouldn't learn what we need to know to make it right.

Here's what we've learned so far:

Humans are built to be social.

Matthew Lieberman in his book "Social" argues, "... our brains are built to practice thinking about the social world and our place in it." Our survival depends on the group we associate with. We learn best in groups where the free exchange of ideas happens naturally, and within context. I come to the group with a hunting problem: Hunting by myself means I have to stalk game for hours and don't always get close enough for a shot: very inefficient, and not all that effective. Solution: use others to drive game toward the hunter. More shot opportunities, better odds of getting more meat: more efficient and definitely more effective. It's the same today: Use groups to drive us to the best solutions.

We have to shift the digital conversation.

The internet allows us to reach millions of people from one place. But for behavioral change to happen, you need to get information back, you need a free exchange of ideas relevant to the current situation; you need active participants in the process. The question needs to move from "How do we reach the most people?" to "How do we affect the most people?"

In order to transform the way we learn, we have to get over our infatuation with devices that get information out, focus on the process of getting learners to participate by sending responses back, and working peer-to-peer in that dynamic exchange of ideas and collaboration. That is what we are going to share in this chapter. Learn how to treat learners like humans, and not like Data from Star Trek, who himself, spends much of his time trying to become human.

So let's time travel back to those early days and then move forward to where we are today and explore how we can use these digital tools to enable us to reach larger groups of participants but do it with heart and care, efficiency, and effectiveness.

Stories used to be central to families and communities; even work shifts had their story cultures. Before the age of technology, the young gathered to hear the wise village elders tell their stories—and not just for entertainment. Stories were used to teach.

Look at the early visual stories of cave paintings, how they gave directions and told a history as a way of being a guide to future travelers. Fairy tales, fables, parables—all were designed to drive home a lesson. Stories were a way of passing on wisdom and improving the lives of the younger set. Our culture, our language, our skills and knowledge were all passed down that way, around that warm fire or in the fields while working side-by-side.

Then something changed. We stopped telling those kinds of stories and sharing our ideas in small groups; we became part of a more efficient system where one person would broadcast to the many: the lecture was born, and with it, the classroom. We had to listen and take notes and pass tests based on how well we memorized the new information. A lesson morphed from being something you learned in order to change your behavior, to something you memorized to get a grade.

And now, the classroom is changing. It, too, was a good idea when you had one smart person who could sit and discuss ideas with a few students in a round of self-discovery such as the Socratic model. But it morphed into a passive arrangement with students listening, not participating. So how do we go back to the Socratic model of exchange and expand the model to include more learners in far-flung places, while encouraging individual curiosity, engagement, and a quest for meaning and insight, meaningful to that person and his or her peers?

Technology can do more for learning:

- While technology does allow information to be delivered to the masses simultaneously, it is also excellent at bringing individuals together no matter where we are.

- While technology allows us to deliver knowledge efficiently and at low cost to many people, it also allows us to deliver high-quality learning in virtual experiences.

- While it often seems to be a cold flat medium, it also allows us to tell stories that add meaning and wonder to our thinking processes and emotional responses, recreating a digital version of the campfire.

- Technology enables us to be co-creators of knowledge and meaning.

- While the technology sits on our desk or lap, it can also take us to the far edge of the universe and all points in between.

It's all a question of imagination and its application, of understanding what is possible. We can bring the campfire and the paintings on the walls back into our lives and share them with a lot of people. We can bring learners together from many parts of the world for a free exchange of ideas and collaboration; we can move learning out of the classroom and into the heart and life of work; we can bring the wonder of exploration back into how we learn with and from each other—when we need it. We have the ability to be efficient; we now better understand how the brain works; and if we bring the art of learning together with these new realities, we will bring about the digital revolution in a way that benefits us all. We can create a larger, more diverse, and more distributed campfire with new voices adding to the telling of stories and contributing to the search for meaning.

That is the potential of the digital revolution.

Four Elements of Learning

We believe that by combining artistic creation, the science of learning, communication, and networking technologies with an ever-expanding knowledge and experience base we can create distributed or virtual learning programs that are truly engaging, that is, thought provoking in order to change the way we understand, live in, and work in our world.

Artistic creation allows us to engage learners in a way that provokes their imagination and makes them available to explore new ideas and skills and motivate them to learn. This happens through the art of movie production and story telling. For us, the idea of a learning movie, streamed to our smart devices, is the digital equivalent of the campfire. The processes that follow represent the conversations and sense making inspired by the story. Vicarious experiences create a safe laboratory for participants to experience different behaviors, points of view, and ways of conversing. Vicarious experiences teach by involving participants on an emotional level where they explore their motivations, their values, question decisions they've made in the past, and embolden them to make better decisions in the future. There are numerous examples of this, perhaps the most dramatic being Miguel Sabido motivating over a quarter-million Mexicans to become literate, not through speeches, but through a weekly soap opera.

The science of learning, based on advances in brain science from research with fMRI technology, helps us better understand the way the brain processes all the information made available through our senses. This science provides us with clues as to how better to create learning designs and interventions that allow the brain to organize and interact with the sensory inputs that we can create and the learning processes that allow the brain to more easily engage and process those inputs into memorable events and experiences. It also warns us to be aware of how easy it is to create unwanted distractions that disturb learning. Lieberman's work also suggests that we should engage the "social" aspect of the brain to better promote learning, by promoting social connections within the class and presenting learning when possible in social contexts, rather than by simply asking learners to remember new knowledge.

Knowledge and learning content are ever expanding and available everywhere to us, yet in learning institutions we constrain it within the walls of our classrooms. We come across many subject-matter experts who are looking for new ways to share their knowledge to wider groups of people in more imaginative and productive ways than the classroom lecture or online text offer. We believe the imaginative use of technology and good learning designs is the answer to subject matter experts (SME) looking for more effective ways of teaching their content. Digital tools and new learning modalities also allow us to think differently about the politics of content and who owns it. Virtual crowdsourcing within organizations allows rapid input on beta tests. Smartphones allow instant uploads of onsite experiences; and online, closed social media discussions across time zones can problem solve challenges between divisions.

Technology, both its hardware and software, are transforming our lives. The challenge it offers is to enable us to see the way we interact with each other and available knowledge in new, and at the same time, old ways. Who can forget the lessons on gravity presented to school kids around the world while by Commander Hadfield of the Canadian Space Agency on the International Space Station? Technology can recreate the campfire for our story telling with us sitting thousands of miles apart, in space, or on an airliner at 38,000 feet.

SCAT Learning Approach

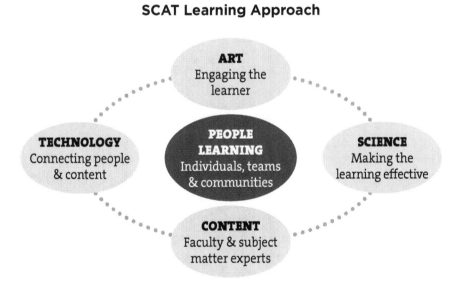

These four elements of learning, when thoughtfully combined, allow us to create rich and rewarding socially interactive learning programs for our learners no matter where they are or whatever their need. Note that people are at the heart of the model, not the technology or the content, but the people learning, teaching, and collaborating.

Everything else is a tool, albeit with very exciting possibilities.

A Structured Order

The most effective learning has to be in a thoughtful structured order, with enough space between the explanation sessions, so that the learner can practice the new ideas and skills within his or her world and then share with fellow learners. Here are the building blocks, in a basic order. Note that every learning design is different, and great attention must be given to the details of the design for it to be truly effective. So this is a starting point.

The Learning Parable. We start with a short and purposeful learning movie that tells the parable; seeing vicariously how a protagonist navigates a new situation provides a framework for discussion. As humans, we have always needed archetypes to learn from, to live through without risk, before we make decisions. Learning takes place when we throw ourselves into a parallel world where we can examine our values and motivations, and reason with coworkers, superiors, customers, and vendors with minimal consequences yet maximum insights. (Think of it as vicarious trial and error.) With these new insights and openness, we are ready to learn new skills and behaviors.

Learning parables must be created that are relevant to the insights that need to be adopted based on the learning strategy. The power of storytelling and metaphor can then be deployed to inspire and challenge current beliefs and certainties, and to create an emotional connection to shared values between organizations and individuals. Once this is accomplished, learning hard skills and knowledge—new leadership practices, protocols, and behaviors—is accelerated.

The Lesson of the Parable. Once we are motivated to learn, how efficiently we absorb new material depends on how it is delivered, how often it is repeated, how much space is allowed between learning experiences, how much trial and error are afforded, and how much deliberate practice we require.

New studies in neuroscience bear out what most of us intuitively know already: that emotional experiences sink deeper into our memory than mundane experiences, and that the use of video to communicate on a visual and auditory level is more effective than auditory or visual alone. But we also need to stimulate the learner to rationalize what has been learnt emotionally, in order for this new learning to become a part of the learner's memory and way of life.

Take the major themes of the parable, explore them deeper, add charts, discussions, animations, and practice assignments in the work situation. Reflect upon their effects, and develop deep and meaningful insights that will inform future practice, as well as develop a community effect. Follow each movie with points that can be inferred by the story that are close to the situation and experience of those learning. Theories, models, frameworks, tools and new skills are now introduced by the subject-matter expert or learning guide. These help translate the parable into the reality of the learner and aid a deeper understanding and move the learner towards change and new practice. They use metaphorical language from the story, which makes them much easier to store. (Think of the lessons in the movie as new folders in the brain.) Recent brain science studies tell us that in order for the senses (in this case visual and auditory) to be processed by the learner's brain into learning, it has to engage the "working memory." This is best achieved when the learning design causes the learner to consciously organize this sensory input into a schema or framework, compares it with other memories and offers new meaning for that learner. Now it can be stored in the long-term memory and accessed again at a later time. Thus, the learning movie and its lessons are designed to be easily processed in the working memory and filed in long-term memory; the new knowledge and skills now have a memorable place to reside, making their retrieval and modification much more accessible.

Multiple Modes of Access and Exchange. Learning and application should be tightly interwoven and respect the way adult learners process and absorb new information, master new skills, and adopt new behaviors. A relevant framework must be added, and learners must engage in discussions and share their insights from other departments, cultures, and experience. A wide variety of modalities can be utilized in learning, whether the learning takes place in a traditional classroom, online, or with the latest networking technology available; what's most important is that the sessions be designed to be engaging and challenging, intensely focused, and spaced into modules that provide a guided learning journey full of exploration, trial and error, and sharing. Whatever you call it: blended learning, asynchronous or distance learning; the principles are the same. Learners need to work in groups of peers, be free to exchange ideas and try on new models, get input while they are at work, and have access anytime to new concepts online.

Most important, *knowing* needs to be translated into doing. With the help of cohorts and coaches, learners need to practice their new skills in non-threatening situations, receive evaluations, observe themselves in action, and make adjustments and practice until the new skills and behaviors are second nature. This deliberate practice is crucial to success; it can be done in face-to-face sessions, virtual presentations, self-created videos, even games.

The Impact of the Digital Revolution

What new ways of learning does the digital revolution bring? The simplest example is the difference between a book and an e-book. Reading a new work of literature in print is rewarding in itself. The words form images in your mind and you find yourself living in the protagonist's world. But suppose there is a description you are familiar with but may not fully understand: *vale of tears.* It sounds wonderfully poetic as our hero passes through a *valley of sorrows* at the end of her journey. But if you want to really understand it, you have to scrounge about in your dictionary, which hardly any of us do. But with an e-book, you simply highlight the phrase and click *Lookup,* and instantly you learn that *vale* is a spoken farewell, which in Latin literally means: *be well! be strong!*

Now the added meaning gives the phrase much more depth, more imagery, more emotion, *and* more staying power in the brain. (Our hero is at battle with herself, torn between the weakness of leaving and the desire to be strong.) Learning at the time of context is far more memorable (and interesting) than learning for rote's sake.

Digital also allows for greater proximity to the source. Learners far-flung can now access lessons, documentaries, lectures, and learning groups online. They can access videos and ask questions via smartphone.

The digital revolution is removing barriers, but at the same time requiring learners to be more cynical about their online sources—checking and double-checking for accuracy.

We've all heard the adage: *Just because it's on the Internet doesn't mean it's true.* In fact, ideas are more susceptible to groupthink online simply because they do travel so fast. It's incumbent on the learner to research multiple points of view and check sources, which enriches the learning experience, too.

Adult and Natural Learning

Humans are natural learners; it's how we survive. Learning is life long; yet as we age we measure new ideas against old experiences—a way of checking answers. Adults are also social and learn much by the groups they move within. They have stories to tell and experiences to share and a desire to tell them. Those involved in adult learning should use these learning methods to create the motivation within learners to contribute their wealth of experience to the whole community. Learners should be challenged to explore their previous experiences, gain exposure to new experiences, and then review and compare the old with the new in order to seek new ways of understanding their life and work situation, and to find new ways of solving today's problems and opportunities.

Technology as Enabler, Not Master of Learning

The most effective use of technology is as a tool, not a dictator. Technology should serve the needs of the learner in areas where other proven methods of learning are less effective. We are not arguing for technology to completely replace traditional classrooms. Technology can be very effective augmenting the physical classroom, as is the case for the "flipped" class. The point is that technology and the use of the physical classroom should only be used when they are well suited to the learning that needs to happen, not just because we already have the equipment or buildings and conference centers and feel a need to use them. While every skill and protocol is different, there are some basic learning building blocks that are tried and true. These need to be assembled in the most effectual way. Learning can be a strategic tool but is only effective when the way people learn is effective, no matter where they are—across the hall, or around the world. Unfortunately, many learning programs use technology according to limited criteria: because it is cheaper and more convenient. That is like using a hammer to dig a ditch because it was cheaper than a shovel, and of course, that doesn't work too well.

Implications for Higher Education

The higher education sector seems to be in some disarray at this time. There are many articles in a wide variety of journals and magazines about disruption to the sector. Bold claims are being made about how technology will dramatically change the role, reach, and economic model of this sector. This has left many institutions confused; they feel that they should be doing something different but are not sure what they should actually be doing. For example, a recent study by the Babson Survey Research Group4 found that only 5% of higher education institutions have a MOOC, that 53% are undecided about them, and 33% have no plans to have a MOOC. There was also a slight decline in confidence in online learning as a model of learning, although many institutions continue to use and develop them. There appears to be an ad-hoc relationship to these types of courses rather than a strategic approach; this may also be true for other learning organizations such as corporate universities.

Of course, online learning, massive or not, is only one expression of the digital revolution. Technology can also change the nature of the politics of content ownership; smartphones allow all of us to capture and create our own content and share it with many. The internet and social networking continue to morph into interesting and new forms. (For example, Facebook is being used to create work groups and for informal research.) All these and others make up the modalities that can help us understand and design learning differently. We can recreate the digital campfire to gather around, include more people, and add a lot more experience and meaning to the discussion.

We make the following suggestions:

- There is an opportunity to think differently about the future of higher education institutions, this should be a deliberate and planned process leading to a clear vision for the future and a strategy to get there. Many people and viewpoints should be involved in this process including the faculty, students, local employers, and those engaged in economic development.

■ Technology also offers a clear opportunity to be global or at least international, bringing the opportunity for learners everywhere to be exposed to different perspectives on topics of interest to the students and faculty.

■ Many small institutions are anxious about their futures within this digital revolution; they are concerned that they will either lose their way and their values or, disappear entirely. Technology is often seen as a means to get to the many, one at a time; but is also a means to network with the many. This same approach may allow smaller institutions to network with each other, sharing their faculty and resources, to reach new student populations, and to retain their sense of purpose and values.

■ Advances in technology in institutions is often led by the CIO/CTO. We believe that the most effective strategy starts with such changes being led by both those with responsibility and imagination in learning strategy and design, and the CIO/CTO. We believe that the use-case comes first, not second, to the decision to invest in technology. That technology should be the servant of learning, not the other way around.

- Lastly, we urge that we should honor the old, natural, and well established ways of learning and add to those the exciting opportunities offered by the new technologies as they continuously evolve; that we engage our imaginations in finding learning solutions that bring the old and the new, the natural and the technological together in ways that really do engage learners in the adventure of learning and exploration, not just chase efficiencies.

So what is the investment in this type of learning? Not as much as may be imagined. Most of us already have the equipment we need in order to access the learning movies, the conferences, and the learning processes that underpin the movies. The initial investment does require the use of a film production company that understands this approach, as well as the script and story to be created. However, once the movies have been made and once the supporting learning processes have been designed and developed, that investment can be utilized over and over again, making it a contextually rich and cost-efficient model. A demonstration version is available at https://vimeo.com/107549457.

So, let's all retreat to the HoloDeck, sit around the holographic campfire with our guide, and connect with others at their holographic campfires across the galaxy and change our worlds.

REFERENCES

Ho, A. et al. (2014) HarvardX and MITx: The First Year of Open Online Courses Fall 2012- Summer 2013 (HarvardX and MITx Working Paper No. 1), January 21

Lieberman, M, Social: Why our Brains are Wired to Connect (Crown Publishing Group, 2013)

Van Commingo: Arvind Singhal and Everett M. Rogers, Entertainment Education: A Communication Strategy for Social Change (Mahwah, New Jersey: Lawrence Erlbaum Associates, 1999) p. 55

Allen, E and Seaman, J. Babson Survey Research Group, (2014) Tracking Online Education in the United States Raymond Smith, President and Learning Strategist, Modos Learning

RAYMOND SMITH, President and Learning Strategist, Modos Learning, is the creator of Multi-Modal Learning, a model using a range of mediated communication technologies and live sessions to purposefully create immersive learning environments for adults no matter where they are on our planet. Ray was Chief Learning Officer and Clinical Professor at the Moore School of Business, University of South Carolina, where he focused on developing the learning strategy and next generation programs for the entire business school, and where he designed and developed the concept of the Distributed Virtual Learning Environment (DVLE) classroom that brings together learners and faculty from anywhere in the world. Ray has been the Associate Dean for Executive Education at the Fuqua School of Business at Duke University, Managing Director at Duke Corporate Education. He has worked, lived, and delivered learning in many countries throughout the world.

STEPHEN WUNDERLI, Creative Director and Chief Storyteller, has worked in marketing communications for over 30 years, designing and creating internal communications as well as outward facing campaigns—leveraging emotion to connect with audiences on a deeper level. He has travelled extensively around the world, working on campaigns VitalSmarts, Rotary International, Foundation for a Better Life, The National Adoption Council, and many others. An itinerate storyteller; Stephen creates cinematic metaphors to spark inquiry, and interesting narrations to promote deeper learning. He is a published author and accomplished director. His work has been celebrated by EMMY, CINE, ADDY, Communication Arts and others. The United Nations honored Stephen for his work promoting peace and civility in the media.

212

Chapter 10

Framework for Action: The Future and How To Get There

Chapter 10

Framework for Action: The Future and How to Get There

By Renee Patton and Carol Stillman

It should now be clear that higher education as an industry is poised to go through a monumental shift that will leave some wondering what ever happened to the traditional college campus. The potential for disruption in this community is high as new technologies, as well as a new generation of students, come onto the scene. Do students really need to attend lectures in person? Do you really believe that digital devices should be banned in class? And why aren't video-recorded lectures and other course materials readily available to help students learn more effectively and to reach those who may not be able to attend class?

Often and ironically, when major disruptions occur, the incumbent is surprised: Remember Kodak, Digital Equipment, the famous IBM identity shift? Many universities understand the current change dynamics and are moving swiftly to innovate and transform their institution's business model, the role of faculty, the students of the future, and their education delivery methodologies. Others may still be of the mind that modest, incremental shifts are all that is necessary, which could result in their not being here to witness the next generation of higher learning.

To survive and realize success in the future, forward-thinking colleges and universities across the nation need to find new and innovative ways to attract and retain students and faculty, differentiate themselves from their peers, effectively demonstrate the value of a degree from their institution, while simultaneously evolving their institution's business model.

Change is difficult, but we have found it helpful to provide concrete recommendations with a framework for action on how university leaders can further the dialogue to transform their institutions for the future and safeguard against surprise.

Common Challenges and the Role of Technology

Educators and administrators share a common crisis in the delivery of higher learning. They suffer many of the same challenges regarding access to quality educational experiences, the need to evolve outdated teaching methodologies, and the imperative to prepare students to become part of the workforce of the future. In addition, they face skyrocketing operational costs, the need to keep tuition rates down, and a generation of students who are increasingly tuning-out and turning-off from age-old instructional methods.

Technology plays a key role in enabling new ways of learning and new business models required to drive the very transformation that higher education institutions are trying to effect. Technology can support new learning approaches that engage learners, drive new revenue streams, decrease operational costs, and preserve and expand the highly valued university brand.

In many colleges and universities, technology is still relegated to a stand-alone silo, where chief information officers (CIOs) and their staffs are frustrated by the pace of change, the lack of resources and funding, and the challenge of translating the benefits that technology brings to the business of the institution and to the teaching, learning, and research missions. But today, CIOs and the technology function can no longer be left alone in a silo. They are literally the lifeblood of the successful university.

According to the Gartner consulting firm, higher education CIOs and leaders now have the "dual responsibilities of keeping the lights on as well as innovating for a new world. The CIO has to relentlessly identify and pursue the efficiencies and advantages that new technology offers to the existing business model," and simultaneously think about what others aren't thinking about, but see occurring.

Importantly, the CIO can't do it alone. He or she needs the support of the president, provost, and school deans to work with faculty members to lead and effect change. While the president doesn't necessarily need to be actively engaged in the day-to-day activities around change initiatives, he or she certainly needs to take a strong leadership position, helping to set the vision, advocating for change, and providing full support to the CIO or other designated leaders of the change.

Technology also helps to support and drive actual change initiatives: Very simply, it enables better connections, easier communication paths, and more robust collaboration. It helps to create an environment that makes it easier for change makers to share ideas, discuss possible approaches, and meet consistently and frequently without the barriers of time, distance, or cost.

Design Principles Begin with a Vision for the Future

While there are a multitude of paths that universities can take to transform, there are some key design principles that are critical for university leaders to consider.

Having an understanding of the future state makes it easier to plan. That is why we spend a great deal of our time working with college and university leaders sharing trends and technologies that are shaping the future of higher education and helping them to imagine the possible.

This helps leaders to identify key "impact areas" that they would like to affect, in order to focus investment and to determine the type of experience they would like to deliver across all constituents: faculty, administrative leaders, students, and staff. Imagining the day in the life of each of these stakeholder audiences makes the intended changes real, which is an important step in the planning process.

It is important to have the right people involved in the visioning process; many of these individuals will naturally become standing members of the task force that implements the strategy and plan:

- The president and provost, who normally already have a clear vision of the future, although this vision may not include a fully technology-enabled environment

- Faculty members who are using technology today and faculty members who would like to use technology but haven't made the jump. It might also be good to include naysayers who, although skeptical, have a history of embracing change once convinced of its value.

- Chief financial and chief business officers who will help identify the resources for the change and assist with business-use cases, return-on-investment (ROI) and total-cost-of-ownership (TCO) models, taking into account specific state and federal regulations

- Vice provosts and chancellors of academic and student services

- Facilities managers and safety and security officers who can help identify opportunities for "Internet-of-everything" technologies

- CIOs and IT personnel who can provide insights into what is possible and the state of the current technical environment today

- Key technology partners who can share future trends, current technologies, and ways to leverage technology investments across the operation while creating comprehensive connected teaching, learning, and research environments

- Current students who are living in the existing environment

- Alums who have an interest in helping their alma mater to survive and thrive into the future

Identify the Champion for Change

The president and his or her senior leaders will set the tone for change and demand action, but the champion for change will probably be someone else.

While the CIO will likely be the functional leader of the change, the champion for change might be someone else. Consider the provost, the school deans, or leaders of other successful initiatives on campus. Consider who has led successfully in the past, who has rallied the troops, who is liked and respected by his or her peers. Consider someone who understands the complexity of the organization while simultaneously helping people internalize the sense of urgency.

The champion could be a highly-motivated faculty member who is using technology today and would like to see broader implementation across the campus. The champion conceivably could be a former student, a customer of the institution, who comes on board to help create passion, urgency, and understanding of the need for change.

The successful champion will work to firmly establish the vision created and set in motion by the broader team. He or she will help propagate understanding across multiple departments of the need for change, breaking down silos and identifying other like-minded individuals. The champion will stick with driving the initiative until it's complete.

Committees, Task Forces, and Innovation Groups

After the vision is set, the work to deliver on the vision begins. Different universities will develop different ways to create the plan, plan the work, and work the plan. A strategic task force works well when supported by a limited number of committees that are organized by defined goals to drive the overall vision and plan. Weekly or bi-weekly meetings or checkpoints are important to hold committee leaders responsible for key milestones and deliverables, and it's critical that the champion be provided with a program or project manager to help execute against the plan.

Because the creation of new technologies is rapidly accelerating, it makes sense to have innovation groups established to vet new trends and technologies and find ways to appropriately incorporate them into the overall vision and plan.

Student Experience Drives Brand

Brand is one of a university's most valuable assets. Several factors obviously affect brand, but the approach that each university takes to implementing and integrating technology into the core fabric of the institution is an increasingly important factor in retaining and strengthening its brand.

Today's students demand always-on access to the network and the resources and information they need to realize success. They expect speed in their wireless access and a simple and seamless online interface to their courses, academic and administrative information, and student services. They want access to information when they need it and where they can most easily find it. And, they want to attend classes anytime, anywhere, but they don't want necessarily to physically attend every class.

The extent to which a university can deliver this type of experience will define its brand. Today's students don't want to attend universities with technology that is unable to deliver a robust student experience. To this point, it is strongly recommended to include one or more students, at different stages of their experience, as a part of the stakeholder community and to ensure customer views are represented.

Communicate, Collaborate, or Perish

The fact that many higher education institutions continue to operate in siloes is a major factor that inhibits change. Communication and collaboration foster diversity of thought, encourage action, and improve understanding, all of which are core values of a quality higher education. Higher education leaders must be able to communicate and collaborate more effectively with one another in order to share ideas and best practices and discuss ways to address their most pressing challenges.

Most importantly, a high level of collaboration must exist between leaders and their faculty and staffs. Including the faculty perspective and their ownership of change is critical. If this doesn't happen, we know from our work with universities of all types and sizes, change will be less than successful.

Finally, students must be able to easily communicate and collaborate with one another, their professors, and outside experts. To serve a generation that thrives on community and connection to one another, universities must make it easy for students to connect with their communities, whether other students in a class, mentors, future employers, family members, or anyone in their social network.

Technology can help break down the walls that have traditionally existed in higher education and to make collaboration easier and more ubiquitous. The ability to hold online meetings, deliver collaborative work spaces, and utilize video across the campus helps people to connect better and enables more frequent sharing of best practices, course-design approaches, and access to outside expertise. Not having to travel across campus makes it easier for leaders to meet, faculty members to hold office hours and other meetings, and students to work with one another or their professors.

Technology Improves Research Efficiency

For research universities, one of the best ways to attract the best and brightest researchers and gain better efficiency with research dollars, is to have technologies that improve communication and collaboration while streamlining the creation of research environments. An example is high-speed broadband connectivity for large-scale experiments, such as intensive analysis of massive data sets like those used in the development of personalized medicine using DNA/genome sequencing tables. A scalable, secure infrastructure is a prerequisite for such work, and the value of the researcher being able to work in partnership with the CIO and the trained IT staff to deliver on such services is significant for all involved.

Technology can help strained IT staff to seamlessly deliver safe, secure IT services, such as cloud-based computing, storage, and processing power, to the right location at the right time. Absent a quality set of IT services for research, researchers will go to outside sources for these resources, increasing management risk, cost, and potential security threats for the university. Being able to save money on the provisioning of IT services enables researchers to spend money on other academic aspects of their projects.

Collaboration technology can also make it more convenient for researchers to connect with one another on a single campus or across multiple campuses. Being able to find and connect with other researchers increases the ability of researchers to share ideas and methodologies, leading to shorter time to discovery.

The Internet of Everything Really Will Change Everything

The Internet of Everything (IoE)is the networked connection of people, process, data, and things. It represents the confluence of multiple technology trends: mobility (ubiquitous, high-speed mobile networks, smart devices, and apps); cloud computing; social networks; instant collaboration with anyone, anywhere; data analytics; and finally, an explosion in connected "things," via inexpensive, intelligent sensors. The Internet of Everything brings these elements together with standards-based internet-protocol networks. Cisco projects that IoE will generate a staggering $19 trillion in value over the next 10 years. Of this, $258 billion will come from solutions for "connected learning."

The network, which is at the heart of IoE, must be stable, scalable, reliable, and capable of handling the increased rate of traffic from the explosion of mobile devices, the use of video, and the implementation of new applications for communications and collaboration. It must be safe, secure, wired, and wireless, easy to manage and administer, and it must be designed to meet future growth requirements. The Internet of Everything helps customers to accelerate the creation of connected learning experiences.

A Framework for Action

We realize that there are a multitude of different planning processes and frameworks available today. We have used the following framework to help our customers move very quickly and successfully through the major market transitions they are experiencing and to turn vision into reality.

From helping to define a vision and identifying gaps to providing a unifying technology architectural design and comprehensive set of solutions that address these gaps, we help our education customers to use technology to transform teaching and learning, administration and management, safety and security, and research and knowledge. We have found, in fact, that this framework increases the likelihood of success for major change initiatives.

At a high level, college and university technology change initiatives typically include the following phases:

Phase 1: Set the vision—develop a "future-state view."
- Establish a foundation for change.
- Identify goals and gaps.
- Design and establish the infrastructure.
- Develop service-ready architectures.

Phase 2: Analyze the financial impact.
- Define key impact areas that increase revenue and decrease cost.
- Conduct financial modeling and ROI simulations.
- Confirm the business case.

Phase 3: Implement solutions to expand services, adoption, and utilization.

- Implement solutions to drive adoption and gain expertise.
- Leverage new applications and services to lay the groundwork for transformation.

Phase 4: Support the transformation with integrated solutions.

- Leverage new, integrated solutions to support transformation on business and learning.
- Improve learning outcomes.
- Create global opportunities for your institution.

Detailed Steps in Framework

This step-by-step framework will assist with the definition and execution of major change initiatives.

1. Develop a stakeholder community using the following as considerations (many or most of these individuals will come from the visioning team):

   a. Include individuals from the college or university who will be helping to lead the change initiative or who will be impacted by the change.

   b. Make sure that executive administrators are included and represented, whether that is the president, chancellor, provost, CIO, CFO, or other key senior-level decision makers.

   c. Include college deans and key faculty members with a mix of perspectives.

   d. Consider including students so that they can represent the student experience.

e. Think about connections to the local community and include representatives from community colleges, K-12 school districts, and other community foundations and organizations as appropriate.

f. Include key, trusted technology partners who have enabled change in organizations such as yours and who can share best practices and help you in your journey. Expand the definition of partners, including technology vendors, nonprofits, and other organizations that have an interest in the institutions vision and strategy.

2. Implement tools that will drive collaboration, engage community, and help to enable a more effective implementation of change.

a. Consider obtaining Cisco WebEx or an equivalent on-line conferencing tool to help your stakeholder community connect and collaborate on a regular basis without having to travel.

b. Utilize video technologies, such as Cisco Telepresence or the equivalent, for high-definition, high-quality meetings. Or, at a minimum, leverage free Cisco Jabber licenses to engage with your broader community via high-quality, low-cost video.

3. With the construct of the group and the selection of communication and collaboration tools above, work with the stakeholder community to clearly define the college/university vision. To start, ask yourselves some of these questions:

a. What does the future hold, and how will it impact me and my institution?

b. What are the major trends and transitions that we have to consider to survive and thrive?

c. How will I differentiate my university from the competition?

d. How can I deliver the best student experience in the industry?

e. What types of experiences do we want to deliver to faculty, staff, and students, such as the ability:

   iv. For students to take classes anywhere, anytime, on any device?

   v. To deliver a range of learning delivery models, including online, hybrid, and flipped learning?

   vi. To connect with outside experts and bring them into courses as lecturers or guest professors?

   vii. To work with other universities regardless of location, to share courses, content, and professors, thus increasing the number of courses we can offer and the number of students we can serve?

   viii. For faculty, staff, and students to seamlessly access the campus network?

   ix. To ensure a safe, secure, and reliable network?

   x. To ensure student safety across the campus?

   xi. To easily obtain cost-effective storage, computing, and processing resources for our researchers?

   xii. For faculty, staff, and students to connect and collaborate regardless of location?

f. How can our partners help?

g. What are potential funding sources for the work that we do?

    h. Where can we save money and redirect those savings into other more strategic efforts?

    i. What are possible methods to increase funding streams?

4. Identify and replicate best practices that are working in other institutions.

    a. Your partners are some of the best sources of these best practices, and most have broad libraries of case studies that you can reference. In the case of Cisco, for example, you can see how:

        i. Utah State University implemented a major distance-learning initiative to serve students and communities in remote areas of the state, now offering more than 300 online courses per week.

        ii. The governor of Virginia and four separate universities in Virginia created the 4-VA initiative to use Cisco Telepresence technology to increase the number of courses, credits, and degrees that they could offer by working together.

        iii. San Jose State University worked with Cisco to implement 54 Next Generation Learning Centers to improve the quality of offerings to students in the heart of Silicon Valley.

        iv. Wake Forest University implemented a site-wide Cisco WebEx license to increase the amount and quality of collaboration between faculty, staff, and students.

5. Outline major strategic initiatives that will drive transformation across the university.

    a. Clearly define your major areas of strategic impact.

   b. Identify requirements across the community to achieve your vision and strategy.

   c. Define required tactics for each strategy and determine how you will measure success.

6. Obtain broad buy-in and agreement on the vision and strategy.

   a. Use collaboration tools to communicate the vision and strategy.

   b. Work with partners who can help you to visually represent your vision and obtain greater buy-in.

7. Within the plan, define technologies and solutions that will enable you to:

   a. Address the requirements outlined in the vision and strategy.

   b. Impact the transformation process of the institution.

   c. Help accelerate and scale the transformation

   d. Take an architectural approach to reduce cost, minimize risk, and remove complexity.

8. Consider the following technologies that can help realize your plan:

   a. Broadband access and network connectivity allow colleges and universities in remote areas to expand access to education and resources for professors and students.

   b. Increased bandwidth and security enables colleges and universities to consolidate administrative services to improve reliability and reduce operational costs.

   c. A solid core infrastructure serves as the foundation for all IoE applications.

d. Improved system integration and interoperability improve ease of upgrades and expansion.

e. Wireless networks provide reliable and secure, ubiquitous internet access regardless of location on campus.

f. Lecture capture allows recording of and future review of classroom content.

g. Video capabilities enable faculty and students to connect across disparate locations and allow for the inclusion of guest lecturers and virtual field trips in courses.

h. Video and collaboration technologies improve communications between faculty and staff and allow for deeper and more frequent professional development opportunities.

i. Collaboration technologies increase avenues of collaborative learning, with significant cost savings.

Stakeholder Checklists

It is helpful to consider what each stakeholder in the college or university might need from his or her unique perspective.

President/Chancellor

- Connect and communicate with alumni and the broader community

- Show the value of the vision, strategy, and related investment, including return-on-investment, total-cost-of-ownership, and other financial metrics that can be reviewed with the institution's board of directors

- Robust technologies that help attract and engage the best and brightest researchers, faculty members, and students

CIO/Facilities/Safety and Security

- Robust, reliable, and scalable wired and wireless network

- Safe and secure data network and physical campus

- Physical room systems and campus facilities that take advantage of new Internet-of-Everything technologies to increase efficiency, decrease cost, and drive new revenue streams

- Faculty and staff training on how to use new technologies

- Incentives to help effect change and encourage others to become change advocates

Dean of School/College

- Faculty awareness training

- Faculty champions and incentives to help drive change

- Online subscriptions to media

- Software packages for associated hardware technologies

Chief Business Officer/CFO

- Understanding use cases as they apply to the mission of the institution

- Financial implications and leveragability of investments

- Adherence to state and federal rules and regulations

- TCO and ROI models

Conclusion

Transforming higher education has been discussed for decades, and each revolutionizing idea has met with skepticism. The lexicon of higher education administration today simmers with the vocabulary of change. Change is difficult, and collectively understanding exactly what we are trying to change, why we are trying to change it, and what the ideal state would look like when we are finished is a big task.

Breaking down organizational silos is a fundamental aspect of this change and sometimes seems impossible; but defining a vision for the future and helping people understand the need for change can be highly rewarding when previous skeptics embrace change initiatives and become a part of the solution that seemed impossible.

While change is difficult, it's not impossible, and as discussed throughout this book, we as a society have no choice but to change. In the spirit of imagining the possible, think about the type of business model[s] that will be most effective in enabling and supporting the experiences we want for everyone involved in the journey of higher learning.

We want administrative leaders who guide institutions to operate efficiently and effectively with greater agility to adjust to the changing world around us, teaching and learning environments that take advantage of technology solutions to better engage our students and prepare our next generation workforce, and a research environment that allows the great research minds of today to create novel discoveries for tomorrow.

As Winston Churchill said, "Success is not final, failure is not fatal: It is the courage to continue that counts."

||||||||||||||||||||||||||||||||||||||||||||||||||||||||||||||||||||||||||||||||||||||||||||||||||||||||||||||||||||||||||||||||||||||||

RENEE PATTON is the leader of U.S. Public Sector Education at Cisco. In this role, she is responsible for Cisco's go-to-market strategy for education and manages a team of education consultants who help customers realize their educational visions through the logical placement of technology within schools, colleges, and universities. She has over 19 years of business, management, sales, and marketing experience in both small start-up and large corporate environments, including Siemens.

Renee began teaching high school English and French and spent four years on the Los Gatos-Saratoga JUHS Board of Trustees. She brings a clear perspective to addressing business issues and an in-depth understanding of the K-12 and Higher Education markets. She is particularly interested in trends driving the massive shift in education delivery models, new educational approaches, and ways that technology can help to engage learners and prepare teachers.

CAROL STILLMAN is currently a Senior Business Development Manager in the America's Public Sector Theater at Cisco Systems. She works primarily with college and university leadership teams on innovation and excellence in using internet technologies to achieve institutional goals. Carol is responsible for developing and fostering the health of strategic relationships across the higher education market segment and the unique interdependencies with government entities.

Carol currently participates on the ACUTA Higher Education Leadership Advisory Council, is a working member of the Economic Development Advisory Board for the Horizon Report produced by New Media Consortium, is the senior liaison with leadership of the Educause Higher Education Association, and is a member in the National Association of Professional Women. She is a frequent speaker for key universities and business groups, and is actively engaged in mentoring other women in technology at Cisco and across the San Francisco Bay Area.

Resources

The following resources are but a sampling of some significant digital destinations worth visiting. If we were to list every corporation and nonprofit dealing with technology and education—it would fill an entire book.

Cisco
Cisco Network Academy:
http://www.cisco.com/web/learning/netacad/index.html

Cisco Corporate Responsibility:
http://csr.cisco.com/

Chronicle of Higher Education
The Chronicle of Higher Education is a major source of news, information, and jobs for college and university faculty members and administrators. Based in Washington, D.C., The Chronicle has more than 70 writers, editors, and international correspondents.

http://chronicle.com/section/Technology/30/

Campus Technology
Campus Technology is one of higher education's top information sources—delivering valuable information via a daily site, monthly digital magazine, newsletters, webinars, online tools and in-person events. It's the go-to resource for campus professionals—providing in-depth coverage on the technologies and implementations influencing colleges and universities across the nation.

http://campustechnology.com/Home.aspx

EDUCAUSE®
Educause® is a nonprofit association and the foremost community of IT leaders and professionals committed to advancing higher education.

http://www.educause.edu/

Exxon Mobile Foundation
Credited with starting the National Action Council for Minority Engineers, Inc. (NACME). NACME's focus is to introduce the field of engineering and career opportunities in engineering to underrepresented students including African American, American Indian and Latino women and men.

http://stemgrants.com/exxon-mobile-grant-delivers-520-grant-tonacme/

Facebook
Facebook has teamed with a number of organizations and corporations to launch Internet.org with the goal to make affordable access to basic internet services available to every person in the world.

http://internet.org

IBM
IBM is focused on higher education as part of it many specialized market focus.

http://www-935.ibm.com/industries/education/

Intel

Intel, known for its computer chips and related innovative products is heavily involved in education from devices, STEM, and corporate responsibility

http://www.intel.com/content/www/us/en/education/intel-education.html

Microsoft

Microsoft offers, in addition to its popular software, many specialized services designed especially for education leaders, teachers, and students.

http://www.microsoft.com/en-us/education/default.aspx#fbid=OAeX1_eUTsg

Made in the USA
Charleston, SC
05 August 2015